Lord, Why am I *Crying?*

A Christian Perspective on Depression

LYNDA ALLISON DOTY, PHD

Lord, Why am I Crying?

A Christian Perspective on Depression

Lord, Why Am I Crying?
A Christian Perspective on Depression

by Lynda Allison Doty

Hazelwood, MO 63042-2299

Cover design by Paul Povolni

All Scripture quotations in this book are from the King James Version of the Bible unless otherwise identified.

Printed in United States of America.

Printed by

Library of Congress Cataloging-in-Publication Data

Doty, Lynda Allison
Lord, why am I crying? : a Christian perspective on depression / Lynda Allison Doty
p. cm.
Includes bibliographical references.
ISBN 1-56722-234-X
1. Depression, Mental—Religious aspects—Christianity. 2. Depressed persons—Religious life. 3. Doty, Lynda Allison—Mental health.
I. Title.
BV4910.34.D68 1999
248.8'625—dc21 99-38445
CIP

This little book is lovingly dedicated to

Reverend and Mrs. Delton Fair,

with all my heartfelt gratitude. "*When I look at you, I see Jesus.*" What more can I say?

Isn't that what it is all about?

CONTENTS

PREFACE

If you feel depressed . . . and even if you feel like ending your life . . . *it is okay to have these feelings.* It is not okay to end your life, and it is not okay to remain in the pit of depression. But it is okay to have these feelings, because we condemn ourselves if we do not understand that.

The pattern is this: we feel depressed, we condemn ourselves for feeling that way, and then we go deeper into the depression because of the guilt and condemnation. In other words, it is okay to feel depressed; what counts is what we do with those feelings. That is what this book is all about. We will study these feelings and the importance of understanding them.

God has allowed you to enter the place where you are, and you are there for a purpose. You did not suddenly appear there and God looked up and said, "Oh my, what went wrong?" He knows where you are every second of every day. Nothing takes our almighty God by surprise. Nothing is too big for Him.

Stick close to God, and you will emerge from this place tried as gold, a better vessel than ever before. Our Lord not only loved you enough to die for you, but He also loves you enough to stick with you through thick and thin. Let Him touch you. Let Him in! The saving, all-powerful name is only a breath away. Whisper it, whisper it right now: *Jesus* . . .

He will never turn away anyone who comes to Him. Would you turn away your own child who came sobbing to you? Neither will our God turn you away.

Jesus knows. . . .

"And him that cometh to me I will in no wise cast out."

—Jesus (John 6:37)

INTRODUCTION

Depression is one of Satan's favorite end-time tools. I receive phone calls, letters, and e-mails truly from all over the world. Wrenched from broken hearts, they describe marriages breaking up . . . good people going wrong . . . seasoned saints falling into deep depression and not knowing why . . . youth committing suicide . . . churches splitting apart . . . pastors walking away . . . gifted and talented musicians going off into ungodly lifestyles and leaving behind crushed and broken families. . . . Lives are being ripped apart as Satan makes his last efforts to destroy the things God loves most. Absolute mayhem! People are growing dizzy just trying to follow all that is happening to them and to those they love. There just do not seem to be any answers to all the craziness.

People grow weary and stop praying. Their Bibles begin to gather dust on the coffee table. And depression sets in. Sometimes the little things in life, like just missing an important phone call, can seem like the end of the world. Burning the rice, or having a flat tire, can create absolute mayhem in a heart that is already down.

Indeed. How well I remember how it felt when getting dressed was out of the question. I simply could not muster the energy or interest. Even the very thought of getting dressed was overwhelming. I would stand at my closet looking at all the choices, and break down in tears.

Have you ever felt this way? Or know someone who does? Then these words are dedicated to you. I come from this kind of background, and much of what you will read has resulted from hard and personal experience. It is difficult to look back over my own life and see any extended period of time when I did not struggle with depression—much of the time, unmercifully.

The day finally came for me when I was able to make the spiritual detour around depression. I was able to spot its approach and head it off. But it took me a long time and many failures to get to that place. And even then, I still had relapses. Depression would creep up on me and I would suffer before I even realized what hit me.

I began to resign myself to the possibility that I would always have to be watchful in this area. Perhaps, I felt, it was like Paul's affliction that the Lord chose not to remove. Paul learned that in his weakness he was strong; Paul learned that God's grace was sufficient.

But I had a pastor and a pastor's wife who would not allow me to settle for that. They believed that God had full deliverance for me, and they continued to pray until one night God spoke to my pastor that my deliverance was to be that very night. He came over to me, laid hands on me, and began to pray for me fervently. Then he spoke those wonderful, liberating words to me: "Sister Lynda, God has delivered you from depression! All you have to do from now on is just walk in it! You are delivered!"

It seemed too good to be true. Have you ever felt that way about something? Deliverance from depression? I had been delivered—set free—from many things, such as alcoholism. Year after beautiful year I enjoyed the exhilarating freedom from even a remote desire to drink. Or smoke. Or use prescription drugs. Yes, our God was a deliverer. But depression? Could it be true? Could it really be true that I would never have to experience that terrible, debilitating illness again? Yes, I was to learn, it was true.

So this is my story, the story about the little things I learned, because it is on those little things—those little successes—that our future success depends.

For me, the lowest point in my life—although certainly not the *last* low point—came when my husband fell in love with another woman and left me and our children to be with her. That experience culminated with my swallowing over seven hundred powerful, mind-altering pills. I had reached the end of the road. I could not walk any further. I had absolutely no desire left to go on. My heart, utterly broken, cared only to stop beating. . . .

CHAPTER ONE

MY STORY

I will never forget that awful day. To the outside world, we were the family who had it all. I edited a monthly magazine, had a local television talk show, and by some standards was a pacesetter in bustling, metropolitan Atlanta. I was also a graduate student at Georgia State University, with a meaningful career as a clinical psychologist ahead of me. My husband had his law degree, and his business as a real estate developer was flourishing. He developed office complexes, airports, shopping centers, and so on. He had finally amassed the million dollars he had set out to earn, even though he had unfortunately developed a case of greed in the process.

We had two beautiful children, both enrolled in an exclusive private school. They were lovely, well-behaved, and very talented. The house we lived in was my dream house. It had everything.

Yes, to the outside world, we had it all together. But is that not the way it is? How much do we really know about what our neighbor might be going through? How much does the world really know, or care, about the suffering on the next block or at the next desk?

To look at my family going away on vacation in our nice suburban station wagon, no one could guess. They did not know about the long months of depression that I suffered, trying to drown it in bottles of Scotch. They did not know about the abject loneliness I endured as he was away, night after miserable night, flying around in his own private plane, showing mountain real estate values to some lovely young thing? And now, at last, the thing I feared was coming to pass. He, my husband, was finally leaving me. He was tired of all the responsibility of a family, and *she* was so much *fun.* He stood by the door, his hand on the knob, looking at me oddly. I could not stand much more of this. Why could he not see how my heart was being torn in two?

"I have a funny feeling," he said, "that if I walk out of here now I'll never see you alive again."

His prophetic words pierced my spirit and sent chills down my back. He knew me so well. His soul was indeed knit with mine. The only problem was, I had never known *him.* I had only thought I did. From the depths of my being, I longed to fling myself into his arms and experience once again their strength and their comfort. I longed to cling tightly to him, have him stroke my hair once more and whisper those magical, wonderful words that everything would be all right. *Just one more time*, my heart begged, *just one more time . . .*

But I knew that everything would *not* be all right. After several weary, heart-wrenching years of this denial, I was finally beginning to see that it was over. No longer was he mine. I had done everything I could to save this marriage. There was simply nothing left to do. I had hung on for dear life, enduring humiliation after burning humiliation. My children needed their father. *I* needed their father! My love was as strong as ever, but the futility of it all dulled my senses. My emotions became numb as the finality set in. My marriage was over. If I were to go on with this life, it would be alone. Without him.

Without him? No. I could not do that. There was simply no way that I could live with that kind of pain and emptiness. I thought I had already felt all the pain that this world had to offer, but nothing had really prepared me for this day. I longed to go back into denial, where it did not hurt so much. My mind raced back to the time I discovered those dreadful plane tickets and motel receipts—"Mr. and Mrs." on both. And I was not the "Mrs." For days I lived in a stupor, not knowing what to do with what I had discovered. I did not know the Lord then, not really, so I did not seriously consider prayer. I struggled with it all alone and then decided to confront him.

With trembling hand and broken heart, I held out the horrible evidence toward him. Even to this day I cannot recall the explanation he gave, but he lied and explained it all away. Like most wives everywhere in this kind of situation, I believed him. Some of you reading this know exactly why—because I so desperately *wanted* to believe him. But it was the beginning of the end; it would only be a matter of time. Denial cannot last forever. *Lord, why am I crying?*

Now it was over, and everything that could be said had been said. He was leaving. With one final gaze, he turned and disappeared through the door. I moved like a zombie to the window and watched as he got into his car and slowly drove away. Knowing he was going to be with *her* unleashed a well of anger inside of me. And knowing I would never see him again unleashed a well of despair. Death loomed before me like a golden ring. Death, the culmination of long months of depression. Death had never looked so good! I longed to hurry up and be swallowed up in its nothingness. I could not live with the depression any longer. And I could not live without John.

I padded down the carpeted hall, the satin caftan swishing around my ankles. My reflection in the mirror was one of a slim woman who was really quite lovely. I had large, dark eyes that friends said made me look like a tragic Russian. I brushed my long, black hair until every strand was in place. I wanted to look nice when they found me, because this day I would certainly cross over into eternity. If I had ever been determined about anything in my whole life, it was that I would never again see the sun come up.

I opened a fresh fifth of Scotch, grabbed several bottles of pills from their hiding place in my nightstand, and sat down on the side of the huge bed. As I began the tedious procedure of swallowing what eventually would be over seven hundred pills, my only regret was leaving my children. How I loved them! One last look at the picture on my dresser. My pride and joy, these kids. So how could I do this?

In utter frustration, I slammed the pill bottle down on the nightstand and began to race back and forth across the bedroom floor. My steps melted into a slow, methodical pace, back and forth. My kids, my kids . . .

Suddenly the phone shrilled out into the stillness. My breath caught, and I backed against the wall staring at the phone. I dared not breathe. One ring, two. Insistently the awful sound swirled around my head, daring me to answer it. My eyes were glued to the intrusive white instrument on the nightstand. All I had to do was pick it up, and I would be able to postpone my death for a little while longer. Just a simple "hello" into the mouthpiece, and I would be in touch with life once more.

As suddenly as it began, it stopped. It had cut off in the middle of a ring with great finality, and I tugged at the cord to unplug it from the wall. There. Just to be absolutely certain it would not disturb me again, I carried the phone into the kitchen, opened the refrigerator, and set the phone inside, right beside the milk. No more interruptions. One last check of the doors and windows. Deadbolt secured. The spirit of death loomed large and cold throughout the house.

Back on the side of the bed again, I still had to face the issue of my children. Two dear little faces floated before my eyes, and I longed to reach out to hold them close. In my mind, I could smell the soft, fresh scent of

Julie's hair as I bathed it with my tears. Little Joseph's dark eyes, full of anguished question, floated before my face. But this was the best thing for them. It had to be. I was worthless, and I was crazy. They needed someone sane and good to raise them. It would do them irreparable emotional damage to be raised by someone like me.

Remembering all the hopes and dreams I had spun around my little family's future, my heart broke just as surely as if someone had used a hammer on it. The heaviness was beyond my endurance.

With a new determination, I began to gulp the pills as quickly as I could. My children were better off without me. Sugarcoated Mellaril and Thorazine. Big, fat Quaaludes. They were the hardest to get down. The little Stellazines and Valiums I could gulp down a handful at a time. My throat tightened in rebellion against the assault and tried to close up. Nausea swelled up from my stomach as the room began to spin. I must stay awake. I could not take the chance of falling asleep until I had taken enough pills to assure the end. I did not want to wake up to the horror of having my stomach pumped. No, now that I had decided on this course of action, I would see that it was done properly. One pill, two . . . bottle after bottle emptied . . . until I could no longer swallow yet another pill. The nausea was awful.

I took one final gulp of Scotch to make sure everything stayed down, then I lay back on the bed and arranged the caftan around me in neat, attractive folds. Somehow it was important that I look nice and not frighten anyone when they found me. Whoever *they* would be. . . . “God,” I whispered, “if You’re there somewhere, please forgive me.” And with that, my eyes closed for what should be the very last time.

Notes to Myself

CHAPTER TWO

EARLY BEGINNINGS

What could lead a lovely young woman with a life filled with promise to the brink of suicide? Today as I look around me and hear the horror stories of how people—especially people in God's own dear church—are suffering from the pangs of depression, I decided to try to share my own story. Maybe it can help someone else.

I was born and raised in the Deep South. My mother had been raised in so-called aristocracy. As a child I was awed by photographs of her in a wide, hooped gown on the verandah of their plantation. She looked just like Scarlet O'Hara, and my romantic young mind spent many hours weaving fanciful stories around my mother's girlhood. After her debut, her future was sealed by an engagement to a millionaire tycoon.

But then she met and fell in love with my father, who

was a common businessman, owner of a small shoe shop. Against the wishes, threats, and protests of her family, she married my father and moved from the big southern plantation to a small, dinky house in the city of Florence. In later years, after the honeymoon glow had paled, she would remind my father many times of what she had given up to marry him. Although Mother meant well, she had been raised to be a rich man's wife. She never adjusted well to the common life of counting and pinching pennies.

She and Gene (as I called my father) had two children, a son and daughter—Gene Jr. and Irene. He would come home from the shoe shop he owned and managed and gaze with tenderness upon his little family. He and Mother agreed that they had the boy and girl they wanted, so their family was complete. God had been good. No more children.

Gene Jr. and Irene grew to be teenagers, and life had settled into a cozy little rut. Mother had entered what she dramatically called "the change" and became difficult to live with. So it took everyone by surprise when she announced that somehow, some way, something had gone askew, and now—well, hold onto your hats and have a seat—Mama is going to have another baby!

No one was what you would call happy to hear that I would soon be joining them. Mother and Gene were both too old, she felt, to be raising a child from scratch. With time, however, I am told that Gene started liking the idea. He had always secretly dreaded having an empty nest, so I would be a solution to that problem.

My sister, Irene, became my favorite, most important person. She was the kind of person who would "give you the shirt off her back." Irene was the salt of the earth. Mother was sick a lot, and most of the responsibility of my care fell to my sister. When she went out on dates, she took me along. When she visited friends at the soda fountain or in their homes, she took me along. When she went downtown to the movies, guess who tagged along. She really had the right to fuss and fume, but she never did. She just took it all in her stride, and even to this day, I feel very close to her, as she practically raised me.

Gene bought another shoe shop in a town about seventy-five miles away, the biggest town in South Carolina. We moved to Columbia and built a house. Gene put a lot of himself into that little house, in both time and labor. There was hardly a piece of lumber that he had not personally nailed in or supervised being nailed in. My brother was in his last year of high school, so he remained with my sister in Florence until graduation.

Mother spent a lot of time with me the first year we lived in that house. With Gene Jr. and Irene both in Florence, it was just the three of us living in the new house in Columbia. Gene would come home from his shop and start singing one of the popular songs of the day to my mother—changing the name from "Molly": "Just Lillian and me . . . and baby makes three . . . are happy in my blue heaven. . . ." These were indeed happy days, and I thrilled to have Mother's undivided attention.

She would spend hours with me, teaching me to read and write. I filled reams of notebook paper with little poems and stories from the imaginative recesses of my mind. I knew, then and there, that I wanted to grow up to be a writer.

But then it came time for me to start school, and everything changed. My brother graduated in June, and I began first grade in September. Mother sighed and resigned herself to the ordeal ahead of her, putting another child through school. "Just as I get one out," she cried, "I've got to start all over with another one." I felt terrible for causing her so much trouble.

I suspected that I was also the cause of her bad health. Mother's illnesses made things difficult at home, because I had to be so quiet all the time. When she was having one of her "spells," the rest of us had to creep around, not speaking above a whisper. The house was usually dark, and I worried incessantly about my mother. I was so afraid she was going to die.

That first year of school was torment for me. I wept bitterly for weeks, not wanting to be separated from my mother. Miss Guilliard was a patient old soul, spending time with me, taking me to her home sometimes after school. My weeping so much caused the kids to call me "crybaby," and the special treatment from Miss Guilliard caused them to call me "teacher's pet."

About halfway through the first semester, I settled into the routine that would be mine the rest of my school years. Academically, I excelled; socially, I failed miserably. I loved the classroom; I hated the playground. I became an avid reader and wrote volumes of poems and stories. I was invited to read many of these to the class—which did not help me any in my classmates' eyes.

The truth was, they were jealous. But I was so envious of *them* and their easygoing, sociable ways that I never learned to accept the fact of their jealousy. Even today, it is still a problem because of my own feelings of inferiority. So I buried myself in worlds of my own making. Ah, what a lovely escape, building worlds of my own, worlds in which I belonged, worlds in which I loved and was loved in return! Worlds in which the skinny little girl on the edge of the playground was at last picked to be a part of a team! Ah, joy!

But as much as I loved learning, I began to find first grade boring. The novelty had worn off, and there did not seem to be enough to challenge me. The other kids were struggling with learning the alphabet while I was already reading newspapers and magazines and third-grade books. I would often catch dear Miss Guilliard looking at me through sad, perplexed eyes, and I wondered why.

One evening towards the middle of the first spring in school, I was playing with some of the neighborhood kids. It was a lovely afternoon, and I had worked up a thirst. Heading home for a tall, frosty glass of iced tea, I spotted the school principal's car parked in front. My heart stopped beating. What had I done? I did not cause trouble at school, but why on earth would the principal be coming to my house if I were not in real hot water? I stood there hesitantly, eyes brimming with tears, wondering where I could go if I ran away. My mind was racing, scheming, when Mother called me from the front door. "Come on home, honey."

She did not *sound* upset. I ambled up the ditch bank that led to my front yard and on into the house. There sat the principal, eyeing me seriously with her cold, gray eyes. Beside her was Miss Guilliard. Fear gripped me again, and I perched by the front door. "Your teachers came for a visit," Mother said, "and they were getting ready to leave."

Miss Guilliard, bless her, sensing my fears, smiled and held out her arm to me. The principal's eyes remained cool and expressionless. But they were like that all the time anyway; one never knew what she was thinking. I slipped up close to my teacher, and she toyed with my long, dark hair, twisting it around her fingers. My hair was so long that I often yanked it painfully when I accidentally sat on it.

The principal stood up, indicating the end of the visit. After they left, I ran behind Mother into the kitchen. "Am I in trouble, Mama?"

Mother peered down at me as she slipped into her apron. She gave me a large, satisfied smile. "No trouble, darling."

"Then why were they here?"

But she obviously was not going to tell me. She struck a match to light the stove and began preparing dinner in silence. Pouting, I went to my room to wait for dinner. I entered the first depression that I can recall. I felt alone and isolated, but most of all, I felt rejected and left out. And then I indulged in the luxury of self-pity. It was a perfect setup for depression.

Later that evening, I was in my room, trying to do my homework. But I was learning at an early age that depression takes away our normal drive and desire to engage in the things that we enjoy. My thoughts, growing more negative by the moment, included everything except times tables. The radio was playing in the front room, and I knew that Gene was reading his paper and Mother was probably darning socks. They rarely talked when it was his time to read the paper, so the sudden sound of voices surprised me. A low, unintelligible rumble indicated they were talking in secret. Holding my breath, I crept through the darkened dining room and perched silently by the door. I began to eavesdrop blatantly on this conversation, which I instinctively knew was about me.

"Third grade," Mother was saying. "Whoever heard of such a thing? She's just a baby."

"But why not?" Gene asked. "If she's got that high an IQ, she'd probably be happier."

"Nonsense. She would never fit in."

"The work would be more challenging for her, Lillian. She's bored stiff, I can tell."

"She's just a baby," my mother repeated, becoming irritated by now. "She'd be miserable. She's just too immature to be in the third grade. Now let's just let it drop."

My mouth fell open. Third grade? Me?

Time had revealed that my work at school, coupled with my Stanford-Binet scores, indicated that I should be in third grade, possibly the fourth, instead of the first. I was thrilled that my teachers thought I was intelligent—and crushed that mother thought I was "just a baby." I was disappointed beyond words. Not only because I would have enjoyed the challenge of a higher grade, but because

I also felt betrayed by my mother. At that time in my life, I did not consider her holding me back as an act of thoughtfulness; I interpreted it as a message that I was not "good enough."

By the next morning I had worked myself into a giant stomachache. I stayed home that day and the next. My appetite also left for two days and then returned in full force. I found myself eating everything I could get my hands on. This seemed to drown out the awful sense of betrayal and rejection that was gnawing at my insides, and set a pattern for the future. Most depressed patients stop eating, but some overeat. I learned to eat at those times, which would later lead to weight problems.

Take a moment to look back over your own life. Do you see any of these patterns in yourself?

I had always held my mother high on a pedestal. If she felt I was not mature enough or good enough, then the teachers must be wrong. Mother was never wrong. The IQ scores were wrong. The kids at school were right. They treated me like excess baggage and made it obvious that they only tolerated me. I was never "good enough" to be chosen for team games; I was never "good enough" to have school friends come home after school with me. They all had each other, and I never fit in. I did not belong anywhere at school and was happy only when I was embroiled in a project or book, conquering mounds of homework, or writing fanciful poetry and stories.

If this story sounds like some self-pity, you are right. My thinking was messed up at this early age, and instead of learning how to change it, how to deal with these kinds of problems, I learned how to run away by escaping into books and academic pursuits. This experience set the stage for a lifetime of disappointment. I squared my shoulders, took a deep breath, and embarked on a life of becoming "good enough." I would show them all.

No matter how sincerely and stubbornly we may set out to become good enough, or to prove something to somebody (even ourselves), we are, without exception, setting ourselves up to fail. Depression is the most common result of this failure.

My own quest led to years of depression, attempted suicide, alcoholism, and prescription drug addiction. No matter how much I tried to be good enough as a daughter or a sister . . . as a mother or a wife . . . as a student or a professional . . . it seemed that I just never measured up.

Oh sure, there were awards and recognition. There were promotions and raises. There were satisfying periods of making the dean's list at college and marching up on the platform to be awarded yet another academic degree. But there was something wrong, I felt, with every accomplishment. Somehow, maybe, I had not really studied, not really. Making the dean's list was the result of some fluke, even when I did it several times. Achievement was like alcohol: I needed more and more, yet somehow it never satisfied. Nothing seemed to ease the deep feelings of inferiority that ate at me, the sense of worthlessness that dogged my every footstep.

In spite of living an obedient, God-fearing life, I felt so unclean. With the name-calling at school and the pressures to be perfect at home, I never progressed beyond feeling inferior. To prove myself "clean," I began the ritual of taking two or three baths every day. That compulsive ritual would remain with me for many years to come.

"Hold your shoulders up," Mother would say. "Stand up straight." I had thought I *was.* I felt hopeless. "Remember," she warned proudly, "you are an aristocrat. You must always behave like one."

"What's an aristocrat?"

Mother got a faraway look on her face and sighed. "Rather like a pedigree. I was raised to be a rich man's wife," she said. "And so shall you be."

"But why?"

Again she sighed. "Raised to be a rich man's wife, and yet I married your daddy. He was poor as a church mouse."

Personally I thought the idea was romantic and told her so.

"But your daddy is not an aristocrat. Aristocrats have blue blood."

Blue blood! How could that be? Not too many days hence I cut myself to check out the color of my blood. When it ran red, I was crushed. *Why did she lie to me?*

"A B+ in math? Why, you got A's in everything else! Really, honey, you've got to study harder."

"You spend too much time in those books, dear. You need to get out more with your little friends."

"I don't like you being friends with that little Marsha,

honey," she next warned. "Her family's not a very stable one."

"I'm sorry, darling," she once apologized, "but I get so tired. Having a child at my age is really hard, you know."

"I see," I said, not seeing at all. All I knew was that I always got in the way. My head was spinning with confusion at the contradictory messages.

In the second grade I was introduced to death. My father, at forty-eight, died in the night. His damaged heart beat for the last time. Mother fell apart, and the next few days were lost in fuzzy confusion. Right or wrong, the thing I remember most was the feeling of being utterly abandoned. "Lord, why am I crying?"

The other kids thought it was great that I did not have a regular bedtime and never got spanked. They did not see the nights I would try to discipline myself to go to bed at a regular hour like all the other kids. I was different in every way.

My mother spanked me one time—when I ran away from home at five years of age. My brother thought I was cute, but I got in his way. He led a busy, active life in law enforcement, and I was proud of him. It seemed that he was always doing something heroic and getting his name in the newspaper. Once he spanked me—I don't even remember what it was for, but I remember the spanking. It was hard, and I thought he would kill me. But, then, I did not have experience with spankings and did not know what to expect. I pouted for days after that spanking, and Mother rebuked him. But secretly, I admired him for it.

Also secretly, I wished he would make me mind by giving me more spankings. A child naturally needs discipline. There is security in knowing where the boundaries are. Of course, I never let my brother know this!

Parents, train up your children with "tough love." Set rules and limits. And, please, enjoy them now, every single moment you have with them. They grow up so very fast! The saddest words are, "I wish I had . . ."

Notes to Myself

How ironic! All this time, I was good enough—for God! An oddball, maybe, but only because He had made me the way I was, and I had a special call on my life that set me apart. We must learn that if we are to be used by God—and we all long to be—then we must be willing to suffer . . . to march to a different drumbeat . . . to be different. While others may be at the local restaurant, we find ourselves alone with God at the altar. While others are walking the mall, we are in the Word. Our mission in this life is to be like Jesus. (See Romans 8:29.) That means we may suffer as He suffered. When trials come, let us say with James, "Count it all joy"! (See James 1:2.)

CHAPTER THREE

TO FRANCE AND HOME AGAIN

Everything has to come to end, one way or another. I, like all things living, grew, developed, and soon grew up. I had just begun my senior year of high school when my mother remarried and took me to where her new Army husband was stationed: Rochefort, France. Part of me was excited at this new life; part of me was terrified. It took me several months to adjust, because I only remembered my one pink bedroom back on Mauldin Avenue in Columbia, South Carolina.

I had never been away from home longer than overnight, and suddenly I found myself in a boarding school in an awful, isolated city called Poitiers, in a country where the people could not talk English. The culture was alien. Everything was so different that I spent a lot of time crying from homesickness. I had arrived a month late, so everyone had already formed into their little cliques. Again, I felt left out and utterly lonely.

The environment in the dormitory was disciplined, since the school was for military dependents, and everything in me rebelled against what I thought to be nonsense. Lights out at 9:00 P.M.? Make beds before breakfast? Share a room with a girl who snored and who griped every time I forgot to put away my things?

The dorm was bad enough, but then I entered the class where I was to learn the language of my new country. The teacher was French and did not understand a word of English. The very old woman just sat behind the desk all hour, her sharp, sunken brown eyes darting all around the room. The other students were reading lengthy passages in French from textbooks that contained no English. The only French I knew at this point was what I had learned on a horrid French train: *"Parlez-vous Anglais?"*

She called on me a few times to read, but I did not even recognize my name when spoken in her heavy accent. She marked me down with F's, for failing to respond, attitude problem. What helplessness! Who could ever learn French that way? In desperation I dropped the course. I was too far behind ever to catch up.

Those first weeks I cried myself to sleep, longing for the comfort of my own little bed and family. I would think of my lovely pink bedroom with the brass bed and the giant teddy bear that I hung on the wall by the ribbon around its neck. I remembered telephones and would give anything just to *see* one again. To be able to run around the corner to the store would be heaven. But mainly, I missed the privacy! I was sorry I had ever heard of France, and I bemoaned my fate.

As undisciplined, spoiled, and selfish as I was, it seemed impossible that I could ever fit into the mold of a military brat. Yet, strangely, I liked it. A part of every human soul longs for order and discipline. Gradually, I settled in and fell in love with the military school's advanced curriculum. I learned that we were doing work equivalent to the second year of college, and I enjoyed the challenge.

Finally Christmas came, and it was with almost uncontrollable excitement that I headed home to Royan for the Christmas break. Two glorious weeks free of the bleak and disciplined life of the dorm . . . two wonderful weeks in the little seaside town of Royan. Only the relief of being away from the dormitory matched my anticipation.

Royan was a modern town, very different from the rest of the country. France is centuries old, the architecture ancient. The Americans had accidentally bombed Royan during the war and voluntarily rebuilt it. Its buildings were low and modern, glass and steel. It was a gleaming, white town sitting on the Bay of Biscay, which ran right into the Atlantic Ocean.

The first week at home was all I had dreamed it would be. Ken and Mother and I sharing her wonderful cooking. I felt very comfortable with my stepfather. He was tall and handsome in a rugged sort of way. He was intelligent, so conversation flowed freely. He encouraged my active imagination. When I talked about going off to study drama at the Pasadena Playhouse in California, he was enthusiastic. Later, when I mused about studying art in Paris after graduation, he was also enthusiastic. As I discussed my future best-selling novel, his face lit up with encouragement. And of course, my parents never seemed to tire of hearing about my life at school. Especially Ken. He showed endless interest in my studies and life in the dorm.

Mother seemed different somehow, but I could not pinpoint what the difference was. I was uneasy. Christmas was quiet and uneventful. For the first time in my life, I understood what contentment meant. It had been several weeks since my last bout with depression, and I was enjoying myself. I rested and took long walks along the desolate white sands of the beaches. I would stand there in the cold wind, my eyes searching the horizon—that immeasurable line where ocean seemed to meet sky. Homesickness would swallow me up as I contemplated America, just on the other side of that ocean. Every now and then a boat would pass in the distance and my heart would wish I were on it, sailing into New York harbor. In my excitement of boarding the plane for Paris, the sight of the Statue of Liberty had meant nothing to me; I had glibly waved goodbye to her. Now I wished I could see her one more time. I missed my country!

But I loved France, too. There was a real feeling of belonging, of camaraderie with the French people. It was more than just that I was part French; sometimes I mused that, in a former life, I must have been a Frenchman.

There was a bonding that was very real. Sometimes I could merely think about the people and start weeping. I loved them.

But yes, I loved America, too. I longed for the sight of a drive-in restaurant and a drugstore that carried other things besides drugs. And oh, to walk into a supermarket . . . up and down the aisles, past all the sundry goods! In France, there was a specialty store for everything: one store for the bread, another for the vegetables, and yet another for the meat. The meat: walk into the boucherie and witness the carcasses hanging in the open air, feeding the flies as well as the people who later bought the meat. As Americans, we could afford the luxury of a refrigerator. Most Frenchmen could not, and they did their shopping every day, setting their food outside in the cold to keep it fresh for morning.

I enjoyed watching the bicyclists shop, a long loaf of the famous bread tucked under an arm as they steered their way through the traffic. I loved the sidewalk cafes and the happy sounds of music filling the air as I strolled down the avenues. I would spend hours in the train station drinking hot chocolate, eating croissants, and just watching the people. I never tired of watching the French people!

New Year's Eve found me with mixed emotions. A few more days, and I would have to return to school. The joy that flooded my spirit was the freedom to run in the streets, not being confined to the stilted classroom. The Christmas break had spoiled me. What would 1959 bring?

New Year's Eve in the U.S. had always meant loud and

festive celebrations; New Year's Eve in Royan met only darkened homes and apartments and quiet stillness. The midnight hour was rolling around and it was dead. Seeing my disappointment, Ken suddenly leaped up, raced into the kitchen, and came out with his arms full of pots and pans. With a glint in his eye, he darted out the front door. Mother and I followed, and there, for the next few minutes, we brought in the new year by banging on the pots and pans. One by one, the shutters began to open as we awakened our neighbors, but it was fun.

It must have been 4:00 A.M. when I was awakened by loud voices. Mother and Ken. Arguing! Oh no! I could not make out the words, but I lay there still and hardly breathing. It was not long before I fell asleep again and remained undisturbed until morning.

Breakfast revealed a pair who obviously had not slept, and I knew something was wrong. The tension was heavy. Ken was silent. He had been drinking, and Mother was upset. Immediately in the privacy of my mind I took Ken's side. There was nothing wrong, I reasoned, with a few drinks. And I knew how Mother could be. Later I would be ashamed of myself for those thoughts.

By midmorning I faced something that broke my heart. Ken had changed drastically. His whole personality had undergone a transformation even as he sat there at the kitchen table drinking his cognac. Suddenly he towered over us in the doorway, a hammer in his hand. The look in his eye made me gasp. "Run, Faye, run!" Mother whispered sharply. I hesitated, then turned and ran out the front door, followed by Mother, who was followed by

Ken. She slammed the door hard enough and fast enough to entrap him long enough for us to bound down the three flights of stairs and down the street.

We ran blindly without sweater or coat. It was cold, very cold, and we did not have any friends living anywhere nearby. Panic rising in our throats, we just ran aimlessly through the quiet and sleepy streets. Finally we darted inside a cafe and huddled by the front door. The cafe was quiet, with only a few customers this New Year's Day, so the owner just watched us curiously.

There! Down the street came Ken, still chasing us with that awful hammer. It was obvious that he intended to kill my mother and maybe me, too. I felt so betrayed. I loved Ken and had given him all my love and trust. I was so confused I could not see straight. Suddenly he stopped, just outside the cafe. He stood there only a few feet from us. We could almost hear him breathing. He stood very still, unmoving, his eyes creeping craftily up and down the street, searching for us. We dared not breathe. *Please, God,* I prayed, *don't let him get us!*

After what seemed like forever, he turned and lumbered off down the street. With a huge sigh of relief, Mother and I sat down at a little table and ordered a glass of water. We had no money with us. Then she filled me in on the horrifying news. Ken was an alcoholic. Twice a month, almost like clockwork, he had been going on his binges, and Mother had served as his punching bag. I looked at the little woman sitting across from me with new eyes. My heart went out to her. She loved him. She wanted me to continue getting the quality education I was receiving in the military school. But even so, things had gotten so bad that she had had to consult with the post commander. It did no good. "In June," she said, "after you graduate, we'll go back to the States."

"In June! But Mother—"

"I'll be okay until then."

Although I doubted that, I did not know what to do.

We had no place to go, so after a couple of hours we headed back towards the apartment. My heart raced as we crept down those deserted streets, not knowing where Ken was and waiting for him to jump out of some doorway. From the next block we could see that his little car was gone, so we thought it would be safe to go back into the apartment and pack a few things. We would find somewhere to stay until he ran out of liquor and money.

Even though it looked obvious that he had gone off in the car, my heart was uneasy as we made our way up those long flights of stairs. One, two—each step seemed to take forever. The front door loomed before us, a few more weary steps. All was quiet.

But the uneasiness grew in my throat. Something was wrong. What was behind that front door? As though she felt it, too, mother stopped climbing and looked at me. She put her finger over her lips and made a gesture down the steps we had just climbed. Wordlessly, we turned and started back down, creeping as silently as we could. We had taken only a few steps when suddenly that front door crashed open and Ken lunged through it, the hammer held high over his head.

Never will I forget the wild and hateful look in his

eyes. He reminded me of a crazed gorilla bursting from his cage. Mother and I broke into a run and started banging on the door of our nearest neighbor, on the first floor of our little apartment building. A little old woman opened the door immediately and, obviously sensing our desperate fear, pulled us into her little home. Her eyes were dark and intense as she laid a finger across her lips. Although she spoke no English, she opened not only her home but also her heart to us, and we made our abode there several days until the drinking bout was past.

Ken was once again the sweet and kind man I had known, and he had absolutely no recollection of any of the events. I now know that he had been in a blackout, a condition common among alcoholics.

I did not want to leave Mother to go back to school, but neither of us knew what else to do. We were in a strange country, and there were no shelters or programs for battered women in those days. My peace was shattered, and I carried a tremendous load of fear and worry around with me. I truly did not know if I would ever see my mother alive again. At seventeen, I slipped into a deep depression where I lost my joy for living.

Pressure was on to go to college, but I could not bear the thought. The school officials felt I should attend the University of Maryland branch in Germany, but I let them know that, should I decide to go on to college, it would be at the Sorbonne in Paris. I loved learning. But I was ready to start *living.* There would be plenty of time later for college. I could not—oh, I just could not!—spend my precious time in France shut up in a stuffy classroom! I laid the matter of college on the back burner and concentrated on my high school studies.

Finally, May rolled around, and with it one of the most unusual proms. American seniors were graduating from a French school with the prom theme of "Sayonara." My sister had remarried and was now living in Japan, also a military wife, and sent me a lovely Japanese silk dress for the prom. But I was disappointed. The prom itself was beautiful for as long as it lasted. But at 10:00 P.M. we were all herded onto a big green Army bus, rattled back to the dorm, and put to bed. It was a far cry from my junior prom back in the United States.

The next day we left for England on our senior trip. The sights and sounds of London enthralled me, and I got the big idea that I would find a job and move there directly after graduation. I bought up all the local newspapers to track down jobs, but I was just too busy with all the planned activities of my class. Julie Andrews, who would later become my favorite actress in *Sound of Music*, was starring in *My Fair Lady*, and we had tickets to attend. She was on the threshold of becoming Mrs. Tony Walton, which meant she would be leaving the cast of *My Fair Lady*. So I was fortunate indeed to catch her last performance on the London stage.

Being a coffee-holic, I wanted a cup of coffee during our break one afternoon. Some classmates and I marched all over London trying to track down a cup of coffee. But it was tea time. All the cafes told us—quite indignantly, I might add—that they would gladly sell us a cup of tea, but there was no coffee during tea time. Maybe we just went to all the wrong places, but I found this very unsettling. I decided I would not bother trying to find a job in this place after all. I wanted to live where I could have my coffee when I wanted it.

Mother assured me that things were okay at home now, so I begged her to let me study art in Paris. I also informed her that I had the makings of a famous, world-changing novel inside of me, and I needed the environment of Paris to unleash all that awesome talent. I must confess that I also took advantage of the fact that she had been worried about my depression. This, surely, is what it would take to bring me out of it. I know it tore her heart in two to have her daughter set out for the sin-filled, filthy streets of Paris; but, with Ken urging her and my begging and pleading and pouting, she relented. Later I would live to regret that she had given in, but we had no way of knowing the sorrow that would assail me.

The youthful wish to imitate those famous artists starving in the garrets and gutters of Paris dimmed, and I found myself alone in the huge, cold city. I was alone and forsaken, stripped of the virginity I had held so dear. The man I had loved and trusted had betrayed me and taken flight, leaving me only with memories and pain and a fifth of France's finest champagne. I lay in that stark little room in Paris, my soul filled with anguish, stripped, broken, forsaken. My teeth cut into the top of my hand to stifle my moans, and the taste of blood was nauseating.

I felt tears of anguish swell up inside me, and tormenting thoughts of suicide raced through my mind. But somehow, from somewhere, I gathered strength in the next few days to pack my belongings and go home to Mother. I was a changed woman.

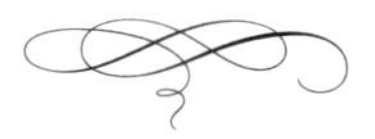

The years came and went, years filled with an emptiness that I could not seem to fill. I was an achiever, a worker, and a perpetual student. But still I found nothing to help me feel the completeness that my soul longed for. Depression followed every accomplishment and every perceived failure. Depression dogged my every footstep. Even after the breakup of my marriage and the serious suicide attempt from which I had been miraculously rescued, depression remained my companion, year after empty year.

Finally a day came when I found myself sitting across the desk from yet another physician. He looked me straight in the eye and sounded the verdict: depression. Again. Even the very diagnosis of depression was depressing.

"So," he said, his kindly blue eyes inspecting me, "have there ever been any suicide attempts?"

His kindness unleashed a torrent of words. They spilled out of my heart and my soul, as the awful confession about the seven hundred pills poured forth. He listened intently and then asked, "And what happened?"

"My next-door neighbor told me later that God told her to call the police to break down my door."

His eyebrows knitted. "God told her?"

I nodded. "And they found me unconscious and took me to emergency."

He leaned back in his chair and crossed his hands in

his lap. "Go on."

"And so I was in a coma for a week. They did not know if I would live or die; they called in my family."

He smiled. "Thank God, you lived." I did not spend much time thinking about God, so I just nodded. "Do you see His hand in that?" the doctor asked.

"Whose hand?"

"God's."

I slumped in my chair as a feeling swept over me that I could not explain. I wanted to give up and give in. Surrender! But I did not understand what it was all about.

"You are a Christian, aren't you?" he prodded.

"I've always loved God. From my first memories, He's always been a part of my life."

"Really?"

"Jesus has always been there for me when everyone else let me down. But I can't really say I'm a Christian. I've been terrible to God."

"We are all sinners. Saved by grace."

I did not understand much about grace. One thing I knew, if I were a Christian, I would not be suffering with this awful depression. Christians are happy!

Aren't they? *Lord, why am I crying?*

Suddenly, I was very tired of being depressed. Tired of feeling like an emotional yo-yo. Tired of the battle. Win, lose, win, lose. All I wanted to do right then was crawl into bed, pull the covers over my head, and tell the world just to leave me alone!

Several good things came from that day in the doctor's office: My thoughts were once more turned to Jesus, and I got sick enough of the depression merry-go-round that I determined that I was, somehow, going to put a stop to it. I refused to spend the rest of my life taking pills or struggling with this thing. Somehow, I knew there was a way out. I turned to the one source that had always worked for me, when all else failed—the Lord Jesus—the God of my childhood.

Isn't that the way it is with us? We try everything in our limited human power to solve our problems and cure our ills, and then, finally, when all has failed, we turn to the very One we should have gone to in the first place.

Notes to Myself

CHAPTER FOUR

THE PROBLEM

I was leading a women's therapy group recently when one of its members mentioned the subject of depression. Suddenly all eyes lit up and all heads turned toward me expectantly. One by one the members began to relate their personal experiences with depression. Some experiences were more difficult than others. Some were deeper than others. But each of the women, without exception, expressed her experience and confusion about the condition—and her helplessness.

I slowly looked around the faces of the women in the circle. They were desperate faces, with eyes beseeching for answers, and my heart broke for each of them. There were women who had been "working their program," and trying so hard to "get better." Sometimes, on some days, things did get better. But they had been conditioned to expect that things would not remain better. Always, without exception and with time, they would find themselves back at the bottom of the pit of depression. There just did not seem to be a way out for most of them.

Although the group I was leading was a secular one, depression is one of the most, if not the most, urgent spiritual problems today. Let us approach the condition from the spiritual perspective, because in my experience, both subjectively and empirically, the answer to depression is spiritual. Anything short of that is a temporary "fix," as my group might have called it.

My conclusions are not based primarily on scientific study but on the infallible Word of God. Life has shown me that God, as our Maker, is the only One capable of truly fixing us when things go wrong. Most of our pain and problems stem from thinking that is contrary to the manual provided by our Maker. That manual, of course, is the Bible. Therefore, the bulk of true "therapy" rests in aligning our thinking to the Word of God, or "cognitive restructuring." This can only be accomplished by the work of the Holy Spirit, which is present in every counseling session that I conduct.

I experience shock after shock at some of the things that are happening today. I see families being torn apart, marriages dissolving, new marriages forming where old ones failed, and those, too, doomed to destruction. I see preachers falling, preachers' wives committing suicide or being taking to mental hospitals. I see dear, solid saints of God falling by the wayside, children of precious saints living in the ungodliest ways and bringing deep sorrow to dear old mothers and fathers. I see hard hearts, closed off to the tender wooing hand of God, lovers of their own selves, high-minded.

Sometimes it seems that my own head spins with the absurdities happening all around me, and yet we are powerless to stop them. God has given free will to each human being. Things and people are being shaken as though a gigantic divine earthquake is rippling through the world. It hurts to witness loved one after loved one enduring such pain and hardship. All too often, the pain is so much that the loved one gives up and backslides.

The more I have thought about this and prayed about this, the more I see a common denominator at work in the instances of spiritual decline. That common denominator is depression. I know a young man who is suffering. I remember the days, and not too long ago, when he was always happy, always cheerful. He never failed to have a kind word for everybody. These days, he is negative. He misses church, when there was a day when nothing could keep him out of a service. He plods along day after day, trying to do all the work cast onto him by others, and getting further behind. His pastor, also overworked, lays more on the young shoulders than he should have to bear. The youth is burnt out and is dying spiritually. He is suffering from depression, and it tears me apart to see it happening right before my very eyes.

Depression seems to lurk in the lives of the infected. It falls upon the survivors. It falls upon the victims. It falls upon the perpetrators of evil, driving them to commit even more evil in an effort to deny their own guilt. Satan is truly roaming about seeking whom he may devour, and one of his favorite tools is depression. If he can succeed at getting God's precious children into the mullygrubs, then he can point out to the people of the world, "Look at God's people! Do you want to be like *that?*"

What Is Depression and What Causes It?

Depression is a deep discouragement that affects a person's entire life and perspective, and for which there does not appear to be a precipitating event. It is not a passing affliction; it is something more devastating, and something that will very likely cause our downfall if we do not get victory over it. It is more of a spiritual problem than a clinical problem.

What causes this kind of depression? There are many symptoms and byproducts of depression, but after all is said and done, there are only a few root causes: internalized anger, sin and guilt, and distorted thinking and feeling. As we will briefly discuss, satanic oppression can also play a role.

In the remainder of this book, we will discuss causes and symptoms of depression and then proceed to the actual treatment process. With the hope that both counselors and laymen will read this book, I will seek to write in simple, straightforward language. It is not my purpose to expound upon what might be called the traditional psychotherapies, because it is my belief and my experience that they simply do not work. I will give a brief introduction to Freudian thought, as well as rational and biblical therapies. After that, the remainder of the material will deal with the nitty-gritty of treatment by overhauling the patient's thought processes.

Predisposition in Temperament Types

Personality and temperament have a large part in depression, and before we go any further, it is important to realize that some people are more prone to this condition than others. Lloyd-Jones discussed two basic personality types:

> It is quite clear that we can divide human beings into two main groups. There are the so-called introverts and the extroverts. There is the type of person who is generally looking inwards and the type of person who is always looking outward, and it is of the greatest importance that we should realize not only that we belong to one or the other of these two groups, but furthermore that this condition of spiritual depression tends to affect the one more than the other. We must start by knowing ourselves and by understanding ourselves.
>
> There is a type of person who is particularly prone to spiritual depression. That does not mean that they are any worse than others. Indeed, I could make out a good case for saying that quite

> often the people who stand out most gloriously in the history of the Church are people of the very type we are now considering. Some of the greatest saints belong to the introverts; the extrovert is generally a more superficial person (Lloyd-Jones 1992, 16-17).

Lloyd-Jones went on to say that the devil can use our very personality traits against us. He can use our temperament and also our physical condition to control and govern us. For this reason, knowledge is an important part in the treatment of depression.

Beware, Intercessors!

Before we go any further into some of the causes of depression, I want to mention one that I keep running into again and again. I often work with strong people who are seasoned in the Lord and in church affairs. Included in this group are the intercessors—the people who welcome and respond to burdens dropped onto them by the Lord. Whether they feel a burden in the middle of the night or on the interstate, it does not matter. They gladly give up their sleep and comfort in order to do the Lord's bidding.

I have found that many intercessors are troubled with depression. One reason is that the devil tries to stop them from praying. Getting us depressed certainly hampers—even destroys—our prayer life.

But there is another aspect to consider as well: too many intercessors take God's burden too seriously. Often they will pray with a burden until they experience victory, but then, when they walk away from the altar of prayer, they carry the burden away with them. They find themselves dwelling on that burden day and night, until they end up in depression.

Intercessors, beware! When God gives you a burden, yes, yes, yes—pick it up and pray until victory. But when He gives you the assurance that He has answered—when He lifts the burden—then allow it to remain with Him. If He drops it upon you again, then pray through it again. But recognize that depression concerning a burden is an attempt of the enemy to stop your precious, powerful prayers.

Anger

Anger is one of the leading causes of depression. Christians, in particular, have a difficult time dealing with anger. First, many have been taught that anger is wrong, that it is something we must not feel. Anger, then, becomes an enemy, something to fight off, something that must be denied.

As we study the Scriptures, however, we discover that anger in itself is normal and is something that we all must face and deal with as human beings. God, as Spirit, became angry and threatened to wipe out an entire race. Moses had to intercede by laying his own life and salvation on the line. God, in flesh, became angry and overturned the tables in the Temple. Can you see the anger flashing in the Lord's eyes as He proceeded to cleanse the Temple?

Did God sin when He was angry? Of course not! The

Bible admonishes us, "Be ye angry, and sin not" (Ephesians 4:26). It clearly lets us know that anger is inevitable and that there is a way of dealing with it that does not result in sin. But of course anger can, and often does, result in sin. It is a powerful emotion—which is probably the reason we have come to fear it so—but one that we must learn to deal with effectively if we are to lead whole and productive lives.

Anger that is not dealt with is repressed, that is, buried deep within the human psyche in an effort to get rid of it. Once repressed, the person thinks it is gone. Actually, however, it lies buried, smoldering like a volcano, looking pretty and serene on the outside yet preparing for an explosion from within.

To overcome in this area is to conquer our thought life. In the mind, all the battles, as well as the wars, are fought and either won or lost.

Distorted Thinking

Another leading cause of depression is what I call distorted thinking. Proverbs 23:7 says, "As he thinketh in his heart, so is he." In other words, not only is our thought life important, but we *are* what we think. As we will discover, our thinking ultimately determines both our actions and our feelings.

For this reason, it is imperative that our basic belief system and thinking process be consistent with Scripture. The Scriptures were given as a model and pattern for our lives. They are true whether we believe them or not. We all proceeded from the same Creator who produced the Scriptures. It was His plan and design that we would all learn to live by these guidelines. They were written from the heart of God to the heart of man. If we break or twist their teaching, suffering results. Guilt, acknowledged or not, is the result.

Guilt

Guilt is a barometer that registers the violation of our conscience or value system. To speak bluntly, it is the result of sin. It can be manifested in many ways, but the following are the most common.

First, there is the *unconscious payoff*, which works like this: If I feel guilty for having committed some violation of my conscience, the guilt somehow "atones" for it, and for a while at least, I feel better.

Take the person who cheats—just a little!—on his tax return. He utilizes the money and proceeds to forget what he has done. After all, he reasons, everyone fudges on his tax returns. It's *expected.*

For a while he will continue to rationalize until, at last, he succeeds in forgetting about it. So he thinks. Still, under the surface, the guilt is boiling. This is evidenced by the twinge of fear he experiences when he receives an envelope from the Internal Revenue Service. His heart is beating faster even as he proceeds to open the envelope.

When he is finally caught and made to make up the difference (with interest and penalty, no less), he feels much better. He is sorry he was caught. But was there real repentance?

Real repentance is the reason God created guilt, and it is the only answer to sin and guilt. Real repentance is an actual turning around, a change of direction. It is a total putting away of something with the determination that we will not do it again. If the man cheats again next year, we know it was not true repentance; it was merely sorrow at having gotten caught. We will discuss this situation in more detail later.

Second, there is *blame*. If somehow I can convince myself that what I did is someone else's fault, I can also feel better. Although blaming others is one of the most prevalent defenses in the world today, it is not a new one. After all, Adam blamed Eve, and Eve blamed the serpent. One woman justified an affair with another woman's husband because the other woman had denied her husband the sexual side of their marriage. "I felt just terrible for Ed [the husband]," she said. "He was denied a basic human right that all men need. She had no right to deny him."

Third, we can manifest guilt by being *passive-aggressive*. This is a fancy term for silently getting back at someone. One man, for example, withheld his tithes as a way of getting back at his pastor. He did not confront the pastor or speak to him in love; he just silently withheld this means of support.

In looking at guilt and searching for causes of depression, we must always look first and foremost at the possibility that *perhaps the person truly is guilty and the behavior needs to be changed.* If this is the case, we should stop at once and deal with the guilt. We should never minimize guilt to make a person feel better! To the man who withheld his tithes, for example, it might be tempting to say, "Don't worry about it, you thought you were doing right. From now on, just be sure to pay your tithes." But if we approach the matter this way, he is not encouraged to confess and repent. One of the most damaging things we can do to a person is to minimize his guilt when confession is necessary.

If a person is guilty of some sin, it follows that he is going to be miserable. Some depression is probably inevitable. And this is good, because it is one way God can speak to us and correct us. He gives us laws and guidelines in which to live. If we break these laws and drift outside the guidelines, then we can be assured that God will let us know. One of the ways He points out our sin to us is in the area of depression.

If we discover that sin lies at the root of our depression, there is only one thing to do if we are going to heal—we absolutely must deal with our sin and repent of it. I look back over my life at my own stubbornness and shiver to think how much pain and sorrow I could have avoided had I only repented and taken care of the matter.

If you have sinned, go to God, confess the sin, repent, open your heart and bare your soul to Him. Tell Him all about it, holding nothing back. And receive His forgiveness. How can we be sure that we are forgiven? I John 1:9 tells believers, "If we confess our sins, he is faithful and just to forgive us our sins, and to cleanse us from all unrighteousness."

If unconfessed sin is the root of your depression, and you do not choose to confess it and take it to God for His forgiveness, you might just as well put this book down and read no further. Sin is that serious.

Outside the Will of God

Likewise, if we should find ourselves outside of God's will for our lives, He will create circumstances to let us know. One of the most popular stories in the Bible deals with this subject, in the life of Jonah. Decidedly outside the Lord's will, he had to endure some tough circumstances in order to get himself back where he belonged. These circumstances could be called *symptoms*. If I were in the darkness of the belly of a fish for three days and three nights, I would experience some depression.

When we suspect that we are not where God would have us, then we, like Jonah, must face this fact and bring the problem to God. Then and only then will release come. Doing so is difficult for most of us, because we have built habits designed to circumvent our guilt feelings. "We pray or ask others to pray for us to relieve the symptoms, but nothing happens. Symptoms don't need to be relieved; sources need to be healed. And prayer is not to be used as an escape from the necessity for repentance from sin" (Mumford 1971, 53).

Distorted Feelings

Depression also results when we allow ourselves to be

controlled by our feelings and emotions. Feelings and emotions are neither good nor bad in themselves; they are a normal part of living, and we could not really call ourselves "human" without them. "Perhaps there is nothing so frequently encountered as a cause of spiritual depression and unhappiness in the Christian life as this very problem of feelings" (Lloyd-Jones 1965, 108).

Or the *lack* of feelings. Frozen feelings. I have been working with a woman alcoholic who never really learned to feel during her years of drinking. This situation is so typical that it has become the norm among substance abusers. Like other alcoholics, this patient had lived in a state of denial, and feelings had been dulled or repressed. When she completed detoxification and maintained three weeks' sobriety, she became deluged with a torrent of feelings—normal to most people, but to her, brand-new and unique. She was accustomed to putting her feelings to sleep with the drug alcohol.

At first, she would come to me in a state of panic, trying to describe what was going on inside her. Of her live-in boyfriend who habitually abused and violated her, she cried: "I hate him, I hate him. What's wrong with me?" Gradually she began to accept that this kind of reaction to one who had hurt her so deeply was a normal one. It was part of a process of change, and in her case it represented growth. Now she is learning that whatever she feels is *her feeling*. It is not good, and it is not bad, in and of itself. It is simply her feeling. What she does with it, however, can determine her entire future. Trouble comes if we allow feelings to dominate our attitude and dictate our actions.

She could allow herself to be so controlled by her feelings that she would relapse and begin to drink again.

Take a father of three children. "I don't feel like working today," he might say. There is nothing wrong with the feeling in itself. There are many days when we do not feel like working. But what does the father do about the feeling? What if he chooses to act on it?

If he chooses not to work that day because he does not feel like it, trouble will result. He will probably end up losing his job. Worse than that, is the pattern set for his entire lifestyle. If he does not work because he does not feel like it, imagine the other things he does not do because of feelings—or *does* do that violate his conscience!

Dr. Timothy Foster used an interesting analogy of an "emotion factory" in his book *Called to Counsel.* He talked about an emotion being sent from the production line to the packaging and labeling department, where it is a given a name ("I feel hurt . . .") and an address (". . . at Jane"). He went on to say that at the factory, a new emotion is produced every ten minutes. What would happen if the shipping and delivery department went on strike, but the emotions plant continued to produce emotions? Soon the storeroom would be full, and you would have to start piling boxes inside the factory. The boxes would start to clog the assembly line, and eventually the whole system would shut down. What I have just described is the general cause of most depression. As the system gets clogged, a person can no longer feel emotions. A depressed person is apathetic. "I just don't care about things anymore. It's like a part of me is dead" (Foster 1986, 60-61).

What do we do with emotions to short-circuit them so they do not pile up and begin to control our lives? We must learn to deliver them, get them out of the factory and to the proper address so the factory does not end up closed down. Ephesians 4:15 tells us to speak the truth in love. That is the key. Lloyd-Jones elaborated:

> Indeed, I suppose that one of the greatest problems in our life in this world, not only for Christians, but for all people, is the right handling of our feelings and emotions. Oh, the havoc that is wrought and the tragedy, the misery and the wretchedness that are to be found in the world simply because people do not know how to handle their own feelings!
>
> Man is so constituted that the feelings are in this very prominent position, and indeed, there is a very good case for saying that perhaps the final things which regeneration and the new birth do for us is just to put the mind and the emotions and the will in their right positions. . . . It is obviously a very great subject, which no one can deal with briefly, but it is important that we should take a comprehensive view of the subject (Lloyd-Jones 1992, 109).

This analysis is correct. Our purpose here is to take a comprehensive look at the subject of feelings as they relate to depression. We must get a handle on our feelings. Lloyd-Jones elaborated:

> Our feelings are always seeking to control us, and unless we realize this, they will undoubtedly do so. This is what we mean when we talk about moods and moodiness. The mood seems to descend upon us. We do not want it, but there it is. Now the danger is to allow it to control and grip us. We wake up in a bad mood in the morning, and the tendency is to go on like that throughout the day and to remain like that until something happens to put us right. There is a great instance of that in the Old Testament in the case of Saul, King of Israel. Our danger is to submit ourselves to our feelings and to allow them to dictate to us, to govern and to master us and to control the whole of our lives (Lloyd-Jones 1992, 112).

Notes to Myself

"O God, thou art my God; early will I seek thee . . . to see thy power and thy glory. . . . I will bless thee. . . . I will lift up my hands in thy name. . . . My soul shall be satisfied . . . and my mouth shall praise thee with joyful lips: when I remember thee upon my bed, and meditate on thee in the night watches. . . . Therefore in the shadow of thy wings will I rejoice" (Psalm 63:1-7).

Help me, Lord, to meditate on You—keep my mind stayed on You. That will keep the depression away!

Help me, Lord, to *focus* on You at all times. Yes, it takes concentration and hard work, because I am breaking old habits. But you, O Lord, are the habit breaker! I can do all things—through You!

CHAPTER FIVE

SYMPTOMS AND DIAGNOSIS

Simply defined, a symptom is the thing that tells us something is wrong. I sometimes get into trouble with professionals in the field of substance abuse when I talk about alcoholism being a symptom of something wrong within the person. Some Alcoholics Anonymous members have trouble with this belief, even though their *Big Book* itself concurs in one of its most helpful of all chapters, "Freedom from Bondage." It begins this way: "The mental twists that led up to my drinking began many years before I ever took a drink, for I am one of those whose history proves conclusively that my drinking was a symptom of a deeper trouble" (Alcoholics Anonymous 1976, 544).

Bob Mumford considers depression to be a symptom of being out of the will of God, and asks the reader the question: "What do you do about the depression? Do you take antidepressant pills and tranquilizers, or pray for God to take away your worries?" (Mumford 1971, 44). As I mulled over Mumford's question, the following came to mind: If these choices of answers were presented to a Christian in the form of a multiple-choice question, the answer would probably be "pray for God to take away your worries." After all, that does sound more spiritual than the other alternatives. But is it?

Let us look at the question this way: If God should take away the worries, it would amount to the same thing as taking an aspirin for a brain tumor. Mumford explained:

> We make a mistake when we call our symptoms "needs" and simply pray that God remove them. Like the pain from a ruptured appendix or the dizziness from a brain tumor, symptoms are there for a reason. God means for us to let Him expose the deeper cause and heal us. Relief from pain could be the most tragic thing that ever happened, unless the cause was removed (Mumford 1971, 47).

The longer I live for God the more convinced I become that everything that happens to a consecrated Christian has a purpose. This includes the horrible things as well as what we might consider blessings. God had a purpose for our lives even before He created us. He told Jeremiah that He knew him even before he was formed in his mother's womb (Jeremiah 1:5). Ephesians 2:10 tells us that we were "created in Christ Jesus unto good works, which God hath before ordained that we should walk in them." God knew all about our personality, our weaknesses, our strengths, and our faults. After all, He is the One who created us. And so He knew what it would take to mold us into the person we needed to become in order to fulfill our life's purpose. That included the family into which we were born.

I do not imply that it is the will of God for a child to be molested. I believe that it utterly breaks His dear heart. But once a child is molested, that life is never the same. The child has been changed forever. God can use that awful experience to mold that child into what He has ordained him or her to be. We are on earth for the purpose of being conformed to the image of His Son, Jesus Christ. Jesus allowed Himself to become victim for us. If we are victimized, God can use the terrible circumstances to work good in our lives. (See Romans 8:28-29.)

As we already noted, Dr. Foster described depression as a *shutdown of emotions*. The person gradually ceases to function. Numbness of affect is common. I remember even today how I went around feeling numb, robotic, going through the motions of living, not really caring about my surroundings.

Other symptoms include a *change in appetite* (either not eating or eating constantly); a *change in crying patterns* (crying all the time, feeling the need to cry but being unable to do so, or not crying at all when it would be normal to do so); and a *change in sleeping patterns* (difficulty in sleeping or sleeping too much). When I struggled with depression, my sleep patterns vacillated between insomnia and sleeping too much. A typical sleep pattern is to fall asleep, sleep an hour or so, and wake up, unable to go back to sleep all night.

A depressed person typically is *unable to make simple decisions.* In my own depressions, washing the dishes would seem such an overwhelming chore that I kept putting it off until the sink was overflowing. I could not decide whether to load the dishwasher or do them by hand, so I ended up doing neither. Making the decision was just too tough.

A depressed person begins to *lose interest in her surroundings.* Diane and Tim had been planning their vacation for eight months. Excitement had continued to mount. But the week before time to leave, Diane found herself dreading her vacation. She had no interest in it. Just packing and preparing became an overwhelming burden. She was a victim of depression.

Once the diagnosis is made, it is time to tackle the problem.

Notes to Myself

CHAPTER SIX

TRADITIONAL TREATMENT: COMPARISON OF PSYCHOTHERAPIES

Some readers have undoubtedly studied much about the treatment of depression, either out of curiosity or because of a need in their own lives. Some have read about the traditional psychotherapies and perhaps have even tried some of them out of desperation, only to find themselves still in the same mess. At this point, they may have begun to give up on themselves. After being a "failure" with the great doctors, the next logical step is to become discouraged and feel hopeless. For this reason, we will talk briefly about some of these therapies. (If this is not one of your interests, feel free to skip this chapter.)

The truth is that traditional psychotherapies have failed us. Probably even Sigmund Freud would be horrified if he could see the havoc and destruction his philosophies have created. Let us look for a moment at what he taught about guilt within his structure of *id*, *ego*, and *superego*. The id represents our biological needs and instincts—the things we want to do. The superego is our conscience, a built-in control mechanism. It tells us whether we can or cannot do those things the id wants to do. The ego refers to the self. It feels the conflict and the guilt when the id goes against the superego and does what it wants to do anyway. The ego serves as mediator between the id and the outer world, and the id and the superego.

Basically, the problem, as Freud saw it, was somehow to get around this problem by removing the old-fashioned restrictions. He called this "adjusting." Guilt, as he saw it, was a burdensome thing that warped us because it thwarted our desires, and his solution was simply to remove it. Mumford gave us an example from his own life of this kind of psychological manipulation:

> In the Navy I had a shipmate who was about to crack up. As the ship's medic I took him to the base psychiatrist in Japan. He spent about 45 minutes in the doctor's office. When he came out he said, "Bob, do you know what the doctor told me? He said for me to go ashore, get me the best prostitute in Japan, get cockeyed drunk, and I'd be all right in the morning."
>
> My friend took the doctor's advice. Did his guilt feelings increase or decrease? Two months later he had a total breakdown on board ship. With a loaded gun he retreated to a forward hold and had to be removed by force and committed to

> a mental institution. He did not need to adjust his superego disciplines to the animal drives of his id. Rather, he needed his id transformed by the power of God. Sad to say, this is the one thing the psychiatrist deemed impossible. As a Freudian theorist, he read the symptom as the cause and prescribed "adjustment" as the cure, when what my shipmate really needed was a good old-fashioned dose of repentance (Mumford 1971, 48).

As a student of psychology in humanistic universities, I discovered a tremendous disparity when I became a Christian. The gulf between the self-willed and self-filled psychotherapies I had been taught and the new life that the Lord Jesus taught was unbridgeable, as far as I could tell. So not too long after becoming a Christian, unable to reconcile the two, I switched fields.

Over time, though, I began to realize that abandoning the work for which I had trained and prepared was not the answer. Indeed, there was more of a need than ever for trained counselors who also knew and stood upon the Word of God. Today's world sorely needs Christian, biblical counselors. I coveted wise counsel but found myself alone in these struggles. Pastors and friends whom I was close to had decided to throw the baby out with the bath water and were not open even to discussing the matter. So I decided to pray and let God lead.

Returning to the field, I found myself drawn to one of the theories that I felt held the most hope, called *reality therapy*. Developed by William Glasser, reality therapy emphasizes the client's ability to resolve his difficulties through rational processes. Glasser also believed that clients are responsible for their own behavior and that they are able to govern their lives by using three basic R's: right, responsibility, and reality.

Right refers to Glasser's belief that there is an accepted standard or norm against which we can compare behavior. *Responsibility* is being able to meet personal needs without interfering with others. *Reality* means that there is a real world and people must fulfill their needs within that framework. It is refreshing that Glasser saw reality not as subjective but rather a hard and measurable outside structure of facts.

Glasser viewed the counseling process as a rational one, one where the counselor takes an active rather than passive role. The client is happy or unhappy because of his own behavior and decisions, not because of some outside events. Responsible behavior is the key to happiness. Glasser focused on behavior rather than feelings, and on the present rather than past events (Hansen, Stevic, and Warner 1977, 197).

I could engage in reality therapy using the Word of God as my external measuring stick, and I was fairly comfortable with this method. I still felt, however, that there was more.

Albert Ellis, developer of *rational-emotive therapy* (RET), approached counseling on the assumption that most people in our society develop many irrational ways of thinking. These irrational thoughts lead to irrational or inappropriate behavior. Therefore, counseling must help people recognize these irrational beliefs and change them into more rational ones. RET, however, conflicted with my basic belief system in that Ellis's position is a more existential view where individuals are expected and presumed capable of establishing their own criteria of right and wrong (Hansen, Stevic, and Warner 1977, 209). It appears that Ellis could very well persuade clients to develop their own subjective criteria of right and wrong and quit listening to anyone else. This is the very kind of thing that has gotten so many people into trouble in the first place.

But I am a disciple of neither Glasser nor Ellis. Their systems are based solely on man. They begin and end with man. They leave out God and His standards. This cannot be. Christians must rely on the Scriptures to learn how God says to handle situations. Christians must also rely on the work of the Holy Spirit. My own brand of counseling became eclectic over the years, borrowing what I perceived to be the best from what was available. And yet there are disadvantages to this approach also, because it is difficult for eclectic counselors to acquire the expertise that is so necessary for effective counseling.

Realizing this, I soon settled into *cognitive therapy*. Its philosophy is sound and mostly in accord with mine, as I believe that one's basic, or core, beliefs are at the bottom of irrational, distorted thinking; and this thinking, of course, was what led to the distorted feelings that were at the bottom of so much distress. Cognitive therapy, in a quick and straightforward method, is designed to root out these deep-seated, erroneous beliefs and plant new and realistic ones in their place. Working at the surface, uncovering automatic thinking was the best way to get to the basic problem, like peeling an onion.

I remain a believer in cognitive counseling, for without a doubt, our thinking must be changed. *But we can change our thinking all day long, yet if it is not made to conform to the Word of God, what good is it?* I also came to believe that confrontation of the client was in accordance with the Word of God, while cognitive counseling relies on a more collaborative structure. Confrontation of a Christian in denial, who already knows what the Word of God has to say about his or her situation, does shorten the therapeutic process. Finally, then, in answer to prayer the Lord led me to *nouthetic counseling* as taught by Jay Adams.

Nouthetic counseling arises out of a condition in the counselee that God wants changed. The fundamental purpose of nouthetic confrontation is *to effect personality and behavioral change.* Specific biblical instances of nouthetic activity are Nathan's confrontation of David after his sin and Christ's restoration of Peter after His resurrection. The failure to confront nouthetically may be seen in the blameworthy behavior of Eli in not dealing with his sinful sons, recorded in I Samuel 3:13 (Adams 1970, 45-46).

When we study Eli and the way he mismanaged his sons, we see the importance of nouthetic confrontation. Eli asked his sons, "Why do ye such things? for I hear of your evil dealings by all this people" (I Samuel 2:23). His stress upon "why" may indicate one of his failures as a father. It was not his business to speculate about the causes of his sons' wicked deeds beyond what he already knew—that they were sinners. It was his task to stop them. Too great an emphasis upon "why" may indicate an attempt to find extenuating reasons for excusing conduct that otherwise must be described as sinful. Eli would have done better to emphasize "what" instead. If he had compared the behavior itself to God's standards, he might have been able to help his boys (Adams, 48).

Adams pointed out that real counseling involves the imparting of information and giving advice. The Holy Spirit uses counselors to right wrongs by the application of God's Word to human problems (Adams, 61).

When I first began to work with nouthetic counseling, I grew concerned about my own qualifications—or lack of them. I worried that my background of humanistic university training would be a liability rather than an asset. Dr. Adams had written that "a good seminary education rather than medical school or a degree in clinical psychology, is the most fitting background" (Adams, 61). I began to see that as true, so I enrolled in a Bible college program and proceeded to study the Word of God anew from this perspective.

God has methodically, patiently, lovingly brought me from the work of clinical psychology to absolute dependence upon Him and His resources for whatever the need. It has been a slow, tedious process and has consumed long and often bitter years. But I have come to realize that God is all-sufficient. God is the answer! We can find the solution to every problem within the Scriptures. We can be healed of every hurt through collaboration with the Holy Ghost. The key to it all is love, Christian love, I Corinthians 13 love. When we are a clean, willing vessel through which God can pour His healing love into His people, then we can find healing for ourselves and healing for others.

God's tools are sufficient for any need. We do not need worldly psychology—and, sadly, much of what is called Christian psychology is merely worldly psychology dressed up in a few Bible verses. Beware! Being a "Christian" counselor is popular these days. There is good money in it. Christians are realizing that they need help and are willing to pay for it. One lady mortgaged her home to pay for "Christian" counseling, only to have the counselor persuade her to start taking Sunday mornings off. He convinced her that the best way to worship her Lord was at the lake, communing with nature. Because she did not know the Word of God in the way that she could and should have known it, she fell for this reasoning and lost out with God.

A young man struggling with his sexual identity thought he might be homosexual. He went to a "Christian" counselor. Here is what he told the young man: "You need to go ahead and try it out—you'll always be left wondering if you don't." Because this older counselor was a "Christian," the young man took his advice. Today he is far from God, hopelessly lost in the homosexual lifestyle unless God intervenes.

Listen to these words quoted from a "Christian" counselor who has "helped" many: "God's care cannot be felt without a deep inner reprogramming of all the bad conditioning that has been put into them by parents and family and teachers and preachers and the church" (Seamands 1981, 85). My own background is one of abuse, including "spiritual abuse" by some teachers and preachers, but I did not need to be reprogrammed—I needed a deep healing by the Holy Ghost, and people to love me back to health and trust. God provided all I needed without any outside "reprogramming." In the past, psychological methods had made me feel better—for a while. And then either the same old symptoms returned, or new symptoms came, caused by the same deep hurt that had not been touched by the Holy Ghost.

From divine love flow all the other tools—prayer, compassion, reaching out to others, seeking them out, and loving them into the kingdom. What is the key to love? How do we get there? Ultimately, it is through brokenness. We must be broken. Even as we lie before the Lord crumpled and broken, we must ask that He break us again. But this is the subject of another book, so let us move on.

With this background, let us examine a plan for healing that has worked with me and with many others. It is based on the Word of God and the things that flow from His Word—forgiveness, repentance, holiness, right thinking, proper confession.

Notes to Myself

CHAPTER SEVEN

HEALING OF DEPRESSION

Internalized Anger

Let us look first at the problem of anger and what to do about it. Anger can range from icy hate to boiling rage. Anger should be one of our best understood, most carefully managed, and most effectively channeled emotions. It is much too powerful to be overlooked, much too dangerous to be ignored (Augsburger 1988, 53).

The first step in resolving anger is to admit that anger, in and of itself, is not sin. Anger is an emotion and therefore neither right nor wrong. It is what we do with it that eventually receives such a label. Paul confirmed this understanding when he instructed us to be angry and not to sin (Ephesians 4:26). Some counselors have failed to help their patients with the problem of anger because they do not accept that anger is a normal emotion. The fact is that God gave us the ability to feel anger. Therefore, we must realize that there are constructive, God-ordained uses for it.

None of our emotions is destructive in itself, because our emotional makeup comes from God. But all emotions can become destructive when we fail to express them in harmony with biblical standards.

An angry person should look inside himself and examine his heart. David Augsburger (1988, 59) explained:

> In anger, one gets a rare chance to see the self sharply, unretouched. Look and learn. Your anger may be an index to your degree of self-love and self-conceit. Or it may be an unconscious admission of guilt. Guilt that needs to be confessed, forgiven, released. For example, anger is common to those with bad consciences or repressed guilt. A thief is far more angry to be accused of theft than is an honest man. It's more often the adulterer than the faithful spouse who flies into a rage when an affair is revealed. Anger can be far more revealing than even your conscience's warning signals.
>
> When you feel anger mounting, ask, What is my demand? How am I demanding change? What do I really want? An honest answer is like a dash of cold water.

We should not release anger hastily. When we do, we typically vent our anger upon another person, aiming our destructive energies at someone else. The old prescription about counting to ten when we are angry is good advice. Sometimes the desirable course of action is to suppress anger. That gives the necessary time for *reaction* to become *response*.

Suppressing is not the same as repression. To suppress anger is to hold it in abeyance until it can be dealt with in a healthy and rational manner. Repressing anger, on the other hand, is to deny the emotion with such force that it is pushed down into the unconscious. The patient then proceeds to "forget" about it on a conscious level. Remaining very much alive, however, it continues to grow and fester until it must once again surface in another form, usually bitterness and resentment. The dilemma that we all face is how to dispose of normal anger energies in a normal and constructive way.

In dealing with this subject, Jay Adams described two kinds of people, the *problem-oriented* and the *solution-oriented:*

> Christians who are problem-oriented tend to talk about the problem, feel sorry for themselves, start up blame-shifting operations, and focus their energies upon who is at fault. Solution-oriented Christians size up the problem, try to fix responsibilities, and then *turn as quickly as possible* toward solving the problem biblically. In the process, often they find it necessary to rebuke, but when they do so, they are able to rebuke *in love.* The rebuke, though anger-motivated, will

> be done for a loving purpose and *in a loving manner*. The energies of the emotion will be *focused* upon the solution to the problem, not upon the problem maker (Adams 1973, 354).

The energies of anger are wasted and used damagingly when they are directed solely toward oneself or another. Under control, anger is to be released within oneself and toward others only in ways that motivate one to confront others in a biblical manner in order to solve problems. Anger is a power emotion, but its power to motivate must be used, not abused. This motivating power is used properly when it drives one to begin to rectify any wrong situation between brethren as quickly as possible. It is used biblically when it impels one to become reconciled to his brother immediately.

We should deal with anger according to Matthew 18:15-19. Jesus taught, "If thy brother shall trespass against thee, go and tell him his fault between thee and him alone: if he shall hear thee, thou hast gained thy brother." Here Jesus spoke of loving confrontation. We are to go alone to the one who has offended us. We should not take the problem to various people in the workplace or at church. Usually, this kind of confrontation, done in love, is successful, and the relationship is restored.

But what if the brother does not listen? Jesus continued with instructions for handling the problem. In each case the solution involves some kind of loving confrontation. It does not involve repressing and hiding our heads in the proverbial sand in hopes the problem will go away.

Speaking the Truth in Love

When confronting someone, it is crucial to do so in love. Ephesians 4:15 exhorts us to speak the truth in love.

Once I was in a boss-employee relationship in which both of us were under tremendous amounts of pressure. Over time misunderstandings began to arise, misunderstandings that at first he and I both attempted to deal with and resolve. But somehow, with time, this process broke down and it became much easier (on the surface, at least) just to let things slide. I remember thinking, Why bother? He doesn't understand, and it's just the same thing over and over anyway.

At the same time, he was also feeling the same way, so we allowed the communication process to break down. I would try to deal with my emotions alone by pulling myself up by the proverbial bootstraps and forging ahead. What I was doing, however, was burying, or repressing, my feelings. In other words, the factory was slowly clogging up for an eventual shutdown.

The first thing we tried to do was speak in love, but not the truth. In other words, we would both deny to the other that we were angry, upset, or hurt. We did not want to hurt the other and thought that denying the feeling would resolve the situation.

Next, he began to speak the truth, but to do away with love altogether. He expressed his anger toward me and the helplessness he felt, but he spoke the truth without love. I would react to this and began to speak the truth right back, without love. It is easy to see with hindsight that this was contrary to the scriptural injunction and was doomed for failure.

His next move was to be passive-aggressive. He would get at me in little ways, such as giving away some of my responsibilities to others without a word to me. When I tried to confront the issue, it came out all wrong. I was on the defensive. We would walk away from each other wounded and smarting, determined not to have it happen again. Inevitably, it would. The relationship rolled downhill like a giant snowball. Today it is still wrecked.

Another case involved someone I will call Jill. Jill felt a similar thing happening with her roommate, Carla. Jill and Carla had been friends since high school, and both had gone on to marry. Jill's husband took a lawless path and was incarcerated in state prison. Carla was divorced. Both childless and compatible in so many ways, they resumed their close friendship and decided to rent a house together.

Jill was a spotless housekeeper. Carla was not. The first time Carla left the sink filled with dirty dishes, Jill bristled but immediately checked her feelings and did the dishes. The second time this happened, she again did the dishes and again kept her feelings in check. She knew Carla was still hurting from the divorce and did not want to add to her pain by confronting her about this situation.

The next time it happened, Jill left the dishes piled in the sink, determined to leave them there until Carla took care of them. Carla did not appear to notice that there was a problem, and every time Jill came into the kitchen, she bristled all over again. On the second evening, they sat down together at the coffee bar. Jill immediately put up her wall so that her friend would not see her wounded feelings.

Carla spotted the wall. "What's the matter?" she asked.

"Nothing. Why?"

Carla frowned. "You seem distant, almost cold."

Jill longed to get the problem off her chest but did not want to hurt her friend. "Nah, it's your imagination."

"You sure?"

"I'm sure."

But the wall remained, and it grew taller and wider in order to keep out the torrent of emotions that were building up. The inevitable blow-up happened, and Jill and Carla split company. It is sad and such a needless shame to see a friendship end like this. Had Jill followed the biblical injunction to speak the truth in love, it might have gone something like this:

Carla: "You seem distant, almost cold."

Jill: "You know what, Carla? You're right. There is something bugging me. And I see that I'm building a wall between us. I value you and our friendship too much to let that happen."

"What is it?"

"You know, I really can't function too well unless there is order in my life. I know everybody's not like that. But if things are a mess around me, I feel like a mess. You know what I mean?"

"Yeah, I think I do. But messes don't usually bother me. Have I left a mess that upsets you?"

Jill nodded toward the sink. "Those."

Carla smiled. "Is that all?" She sprang from the barstool and dug into the dirty dishes. "I'll take care of it in a jif."

Such a different outcome!

Relieved, Jill would then join her friend, and together they would have the kitchen sparkling in no time. And Carla would try to be careful from then on. When she did slip up, Jill would not bristle. She would have more understanding and patience, because she would know Carla was really was trying. The result would have been different because Jill took the time to speak the truth in love. Doing so is much better than silently stuffing our anger!

Jill could also have spoken the truth, but not in love. She could have yelled and flown off the handle. The end result would have been the same as not saying anything. The Bible way is to confront, to speak the truth in love, and to forgive.

Notes to Myself

CHAPTER EIGHT

FORGIVENESS AND GUILT

We cannot stress too much the importance of forgiveness. The Scriptures plainly say that if we do not forgive, then God will not forgive us. And if we are in the depths of depression, needing to have some sin forgiven and washed from our heart, we are in a true bind. We will be unable to find healing. In Mark 11:26 Jesus told us, "But if ye do not forgive, neither will your Father which is in heaven forgive your trespasses." Those are heavy, serious words that can constitute either our condemnation or a beautiful promise of our own forgiveness.

You say you cannot forgive? Then let me suggest to you a way. Picture in your mind the following: You worked late at the office and when you leave your building to head for your car, everything is dark and deserted. You pause for a moment as you leave your office building. Not a soul is around. Your car is the only one in the parking lot across the street, and suddenly it seems like a long, long way.

You square your shoulders, sigh, and cross the street to the parking lot. You quicken your pace and begin to regret ever working so late in the first place. Your heels click on the pavement as you cross the deserted parking lot. Suddenly, from out of the shadowed mist, a man steps out and begins walking toward you. An eerie chill crawls up your spine and your pace falters. You wonder what to do. You stop dead still. He continues to walk.

As he gets closer you notice his unkempt look, long hair, and scraggly beard. Then he is just a few steps from you. He stops. Tattoos glare at you from his muscular triceps. His eyes look at you, glistening, crazed, and you are certain he is on drugs. You are on the verge of screaming because you are certain he is getting ready to kill you. You can tell just by looking at him!

But wait.

Look at him with a different point of view. Suppose you were his mother. You still see the unkempt appearance, the wild look in his eyes, the awful tattoos. But you see something else, too. You see him as a little boy. You remember the times he cried himself to sleep because a friend had rejected him. You remember the helpless look when his father walked out, and he was forced to grow up without a dad. You remember the little paper route he faithfully threw. You remember—yes, you know the young man as only a mother could. You have insight. You have a commitment to this child.

Try to see the person you need to forgive through these eyes. Look at him as a father would—his heavenly Father. Did the prodigal son receive forgiveness? Did he deserve it? If we can look at another person through eyes of compassion and understanding, we can allow God to forgive through us. We can allow God to bless this person through us.

When the heart is willing, God can perform wonders within it. A situation from my own life helps to illustrate this truth. There had been a deep break in my friendship with a person who was very important to me and a vital part of my life. We had done and said things that had hurt each other, and we were both to blame for the termination of the relationship. At first, however, I could focus only on the wrong that I had done. I assumed all of the blame myself and was unable to see that he shared in the blame. As a result, I had gone to him for his forgiveness several times.

A year came and went and still we were not reconciled. The thing was eating at me night and day, and I began to realize that some forgiveness had to be done on *my* part. I began to focus on the hurt he had caused me and my children, and anger and bitterness began to loom large. I knew what God said. I knew I had to forgive this man. But I could not. I sought the Lord and explained to Him my plight, but He seemed so far away. I would muster up forgiveness and feel for a while that everything was completed—but only for a while. Something would happen to reopen the wounds, and I felt the awful pain afresh.

One night I sat in the silence of my living room trying to pray, the Bible opened on my lap. Suddenly the presence of God entered the room, and He began to bathe me with His warmth. Wave after wave of sheer joy and awe swept over me, and I realized it was the Lord visiting with me.

I wept quietly, basking in the love He was showering on me. What joy, what cleansing I felt! And then He spoke inside of me in a still, small voice: "Call him [the friend I could not forgive] and tell him you're sorry."

I whispered, "I already have, Lord."

"Do it once more. This time accept all the blame."

"All of it?"

"All of it. Do it for me."

The presence of God was still there, although no longer bathing me as before. It was as though He had stepped off into a corner and was just waiting. He had put the ball in my court, now what would I do with it? I looked at my watch. It was 10:30, a bit late to be calling. But I lifted the phone and dialed his number, silently praying he would not answer. A moment later he was on the other end of the line. I took a big gulp of pride and apologized again to him, this time offering no excuses, no rationale. I kept it brief, explaining that I was doing this to make things right with God.

He accepted the apology and we hung up. I did not know what I had expected, but I was disappointed. "See, Lord? It did not do any good. I feel so stupid." But in my heart I knew I had obeyed the Lord, and I felt good and clean. Joy was springing up inside of me.

Two nights later in church, my pastor was speaking on the subject of forgiveness. As he preached and I sat there raptly listening, that joy began to sweep all over me. The preacher asked a question: "How do we know when we've forgiven someone?"

That caught my attention, because there had been many times I had only thought I had completed the act of forgiveness. The preacher answered his own question: "When that person has been restored to his former place of love within our hearts."

Suddenly the revelation swept over me: When I asked my friend for forgiveness last Monday night, I myself had actually forgiven him! Since that night, I have known only the old love for my lost friend; I have only prayed for good things for him. He had indeed been restored to the former place of love in my heart. The power of forgiveness!

The Problem of Guilt

Whether we are working with someone else's guilt or our own, the cardinal rule is never minimize guilt to make a person feel better. Traditional psychotherapies do not work. They use guilt as a method of focusing blame somewhere outside ourselves. God's way is to admit our guilt, confess it, repent, make restoration, and then move on with life.

Once when I was in therapy, I was supposed to work on my relationship with my mother. Throughout the course of my life, our relationship had brought me much anger and guilt and frustration, and I had never dealt with these emotions and situations. Now I was to express them all, let out all the anger, and direct it toward my mother, who lived three thousand miles away. I was to shout and scream, I was to pound the pillow and beat things, all the while pretending it was my mother. Something inside of me warned against this kind of "therapy." I have since learned about our thoughts being such very real things, and expressing raw anger in this way would not only have *not* helped me, I believe it would also have eventually hurt my mother.

Thoughts—especially thoughts powered by strong emotions—are very real. Once set in motion, they reach a mark. Thoughts are very real entities. Once thought, they continue to live. Speaking them is like adding fuel to the fire. What I needed to do was confess those things I was truly guilty of, and forgive my mother for all the rest. She was merely doing the best she could with what she had to work with. Somehow, understanding this principle in our relationships is half the battle. Such an understanding forms a bond among all of us, as God's creation. It cements our relationships, because it is a common bond: we are all trying to do the best we can with what we have to work with. When we understand this principle, we will notice a real difference in our relationships.

Resolving Guilt

The biblical method of resolving guilt is by confession and repentance. In explaining repentance, the Bible speaks of godly sorrow and worldly sorrow. Christians often need help untangling the two. II Corinthians 7:10 tells us, "For godly sorrow worketh repentance to salvation not to be repented of: but the sorrow of the world worketh death." Here we see clearly that there are two kinds of sorrow. The Bible gives us a succinct example in the story of Judas and Peter when they failed the Lord.

Peter and Judas were both disciples of Jesus. Both were in responsible positions. Both had the advantage of learning from the Master on an intimate basis. Both had equal advantages. And both failed the Lord (Allison 1991).

But Peter ended up repenting and going on to do great works for God, while Judas ended up committing suicide. What made the difference? The circumstances were the same, but the outcomes were so different. We do not have all the answers, but this we do know: Peter experienced godly sorrow. The Bible says he went out and wept bitterly in repentance. Judas, however, engaged in the sorrow of the world. He regretted what he had done. He had remorse. But it was the kind that the world experiences. Judas tried to solve the dilemma in his own strength by giving the betrayal money back.

Peter threw himself on the mercy of the Lord, and the Lord thoroughly forgave him. Peter was not ostracized, nor did he have to do penance or step down to a lower position. On the contrary, Jesus elevated him to the position of caring for His sheep; and on the Day of Pentecost, Peter stood up and preached the first Christian message recorded in history, a message that resulted in three thousand people receiving the Holy Spirit in one day! That message is recorded in the second chapter of the Book of Acts. But Judas committed suicide and was buried in a potter's grave.

To repent, we must confess. We must come clean with God and with anyone we have sinned against. And then we must turn from those sinful ways. Repentance literally means doing an about face—giving up the practice of sin and turning away from it, going in the opposite direction. This is where so many of us have problems. It is one thing to admit we have sinned, that the sin is harmful to us, and even to confess to the party we have sinned against. But sometimes, giving up that sin, letting go of something that has become pleasurable and comfortable, just seems too difficult. Yet, on this decision, the rest of our lives can be determined.

Notes to Myself

CHAPTER NINE

HEALING BY CHANGING THOUGHTS AND FEELINGS

We now come to the very heart of our study. We must challenge our distorted thinking to get at the root cause of depression. Psalm 73 illustrates what happens when we do not discover and correct our faulty thinking. Asaph's feet were almost gone; his steps had almost slipped. For sixteen verses, Asaph lamented his poor condition as contrasted with the apparent prosperity of the wicked. He was in a deep depression. In verse 16, he wailed, "When I thought to know this, it was too painful for me."

In passages such as these, the Bible reveals its characters' imperfections as well as their good points. The Bible always tells it just like it is. God knew that one day His children would need to read about others who had suffered as they are presently suffering—and who had overcome. In the next verse, Asaph gave the secret to victory: "Until I went into the sanctuary of God; then understood I their end" (Psalm 73:17). The remainder of this psalm goes on to extol God and His great ways, climaxing with Asaph's pure trust in the final verse.

Asaph was not sitting in a counselor's office somewhere, undergoing a therapeutic dialogue. No great therapeutic technique was exercised between verses 16 and 17. The action that changed Asaph's thinking was going to the sanctuary of God. Even there, we do not read that he counseled with a priest or another person. Instead, he conducted a dialogue inside his own head. He prayed. And, as David, Asaph encouraged himself in the Lord. (I Samuel 30:6.) We must learn to do the same. We must learn to control what we talk about with ourselves inside our heads!

C. S. Lovett told about a time he, Dewey Lockman, and Franklin Logsdon went to see Charles E. Fuller, preacher on the *Old-Fashioned Revival Hour* and founder of Fuller Seminary. In the conversation, the name of a prominent Christian leader was mentioned, one who was then attacking Fuller Seminary. "I shall never forget Brother Fuller's response to the comment this man made about his school," Lovett reported.

"'Yeeesss,' he drawled, 'God bless him.'

"Dr. Logsdon was the quickest to respond, 'You don't seem too upset, Brother Fuller!'

"Then came an astonishing reply: 'Why should I let someone else decide how I am going to act!'" (Lovett 1968, 71-72).

"As He Thinketh . . ."

We can eliminate a large chunk of our misery by applying a simple principle. While the method itself is simple, it is not always easy to implement. It requires that we change habits of a lifetime, and we cannot expect to do this overnight. It takes effort. It requires diligence. *But following this principle will be worth it a hundred times over!*

The wise man Solomon declared of a miser, "As he thinketh in his heart, so is he" (Proverbs 23:7). In other words, a person's character and actions are determined by what he thinks. If we want to change our direction, and if we want to assume control over our lives, then we must change our way of thinking. When we do, our life can become a joy no matter the circumstances.

Most of our burdens would be lightened if we would change the way we look at those burdens, if we could lift our eyes to God and see Him at work in the situation. One of the most life-changing principles I ever learned (and am still learning!) is that I am in control of what I allow to blossom in my mind.

Have you ever had a pet suggestion vetoed? A favorite project scrapped? Has the Sunday school superintendent refused to implement those changes that you *know* will make for a better department? How do we handle set-backs like these? Women typically react with feelings of helplessness, guilt, resentment, and depression. Let us take a hypothetical example.

A Cold, Rainy Night

It is your twenty-fifth wedding anniversary, one of the most important days in your life. You have planned for this occasion for so long. When it finally arrives, your husband, John, goes out of town on business and leaves you alone. How do you react? Do you get angry? Resentful? This is the most important day in the year to you, and you had made big, marvelous, and wonderfully romantic plans. Then you feel *guilty* for feeling angry and resentful . . . and the whole thing snowballs.

You are all alone, trying to cheer yourself up, but it is cold outside. On top of that, it is raining. The weather just makes everything seem worse. You sit there and think for a while about how you *always* get depressed in this kind of weather.

Note the word *always*. That is usually a tip-off to what cognitive therapists call "automatic thinking." What you need to realize is that it is not the cold, rainy night that is causing the depression; it is not even that you are *alone* on the cold, rainy night. It is how you *perceive* being alone on a cold, rainy night. What, exactly, are you telling yourself about this situation? Are you saying something like this: "Why did John have to go and leave me tonight! He *should have* [another tip-off] realized that I need to have him home on our anniversary!"

Thus, it is not our circumstances that control our behavior, it is what we *believe* about those circumstances. "If John loved me," you might say to yourself on that lonely night, "he would not have gone off and left me by myself." That implies that you are unloved by John. Look where this self-conversation is heading. If something is not done to put the brakes on this kind of thinking, soon the self-pity will develop into bitterness. "Just wait till he wants me to do something for him; I'll show him." Here we have the root of bitterness mentioned in Hebrews 12:15.

If our thoughts create our emotions and then our emotions create our behavior, what can we do to create change in our lives? We can change our emotion by changing our thoughts.

But wait . . .

Not All Situations Are Meant to Be Changed

Alcoholics use a prayer called the "Serenity Prayer" that should be a part of everyone's daily attitude: "God grant me the serenity to accept the things I cannot change, the courage to change the things I can, and the wisdom to know the difference." Some things simply are not meant to be changed. Some things are offered to us by God's loving hand to train us and teach us. Some things are a part of His perfect plan for our lives. We need only accept these things, say, "Thank you, Jesus," and march on.

Some things are simply a part of life and we must accept those, too. If John, for example, absolutely must go out of town, it is destructive for his wife to insist that he stay with her to celebrate their anniversary. If he tried to work out an alternative and was not able to, then she must accept the circumstances.

Paul encountered one of these situations with "a thorn in the flesh." He sought God three times about removing it. Finally God said, in essence, "No, this is a situation I want you to learn to live with; I have a purpose for it." So Paul changed his thinking about the thorn. He accepted it, he thanked God for giving him grace sufficient to bear it, and he thanked God for areas of weakness that allowed him to become strong in the Lord. (See II Corinthians 12:7-10.)

Those situations we cannot change are golden opportunities for us to change ourselves—by interpreting them in a different way, a positive and fulfilling way. But we must be prepared to fail a few times. It requires much hard work to bring our thoughts into captivity, as II Corinthians 10:5 instructs. When negative thinking comes, we must stop it and begin to quote Scripture. Or we can replace the negative thought with an opposite one such as "I can!" instead of "I could never do that."

Paul gave more life-changing advice in Philippians 4:8, when he said to practice thinking on good things. Going back to that lonely anniversary, it is easy to see that the wife was getting into a pattern of *generalized thinking*. She found herself thinking, John doesn't love me, period, because he wasn't here this one night. She generalized the one event to include the entire relationship. Instead she could say, "I know John loves me." Or, "Just last week he brought me flowers." And, "He sent me that darling little card with the teddy bear on the front."

Immediately she will feel better! "He's always calling from the office just to tell me he loves me."

With this new way of thinking, gradually the night grows sweeter. The wife begins to feel loved again. Her strength returns. As she thinks of little things she can do when John comes back, enthusiasm returns to her life. Excitement mounts as she begins planning for his homecoming.

She has just achieved victory over another round of depression!

Our thoughts, then, *do* make a difference! The pattern of our thinking can alter the course of our entire life. Our goal should be to discover our purpose by obeying our Maker at each stage, fixing our gaze and thoughts on Him, and then following steadfastly where He leads.

Notes to Myself

CHAPTER TEN

THE PERILS OF POSITIVE THINKING

Godly Thinking versus Positive Thinking

As I engage in cognitive therapy, some clients are struck by the similarity to the popular so-called positive thinking. It is called this because it focuses on the positive while ignoring the negative. I am opposed to traditional positive thinking as much as I am to negative thinking. They are both nonproductive, even dangerous, as we have seen. William H. Cook explained:

> The fallacy of the positive thinking movement is not positive thinking. The fallacy is in getting positive too soon. If we do not get our motivation

> from God, put our "success" under God, we might be in for trouble. It is not enough to simply start a day saying, "I'm going to be positive, I am going to get victory over this, I am determined to think only positive thoughts." I—I—I! God may choose not to add his blessings to our human methodology when the same human methodology phased him out of the planning (Cook 1974, 65).

Affirmations have their place, surely, and we will discuss them later when we talk about Ipecac. But we must remember to include God in all our ways.

William Cook spoke about an unsaved person telling himself positive things about his spiritual condition, and Cook asked the question: Does positive thinking change his relationship to God? Is he now God's child?

> If a carpenter makes a pulpit stand for a church, can it be said that the pulpit is his child? The piece of furniture is his product, not his child. There's a great deal of difference between being one of God's products and one of God's children. As it would be necessary to be born into the family of a carpenter to be the child of a carpenter, so it is necessary to be born into the family of God to be considered God's child. . . . Positive thinking, based on truth, carries fantastic blessing. Getting positive too soon, on the other hand, can do irreparable damage (Cook 1974, 65).

It is foolhardy to counsel an unsaved person as though he were a born-again Christian, especially in relation to his thinking. Our aim should be to witness to him and to help lead him to Christ. Until that time, we must adhere to the biblical principles that apply to everyone in general.

We must remember, too, that the New Testament Epistles address the church, not the unsaved. It takes the power of the Holy Spirit dwelling within a person to accomplish the spiritual goals that the Epistles set forth. Thus, counselors must always keep in mind the spiritual condition of their patients. In this regard, Cook cautioned:

> In swimming, I either can or I can't. A thousand times I may tell myself, "I know I can swim." If I psych myself, if I act as if I can when I can't, and jump into the deep water anyway, I may drown.
>
> In war, I can rush the enemy who outnumbers me 10 to 1, and all the while be acting as if I can whip them all, but the odds are real good that I'll soon be dead.
>
> In sickness, I can psych myself and act as if I don't hurt and I may escape 30 percent of the time, but the other 70 percent will scar or kill.
>
> In sin, I can choose to ignore the reality of it in my life, but much of my joy is lost and I short-circuit hundreds of blessings in the power area.
>
> In success and achievement, I can psych myself into emphasizing how much I can accomplish (watch that big 'I'). Years hence the realization will

> come that I have not achieved half of what I could have achieved if God had been directing my life.
>
> It scarcely seems worthwhile to risk your life and your career just because someone said acting . . . would work wonders for you. Maybe they forgot to mention that it only works in some things and then it only works some of the time" (Cook 1974, 69).

How can people without the indwelling of the Holy Ghost put on the whole armor of God? They must be taught and trained; they must see what the Scriptures say about their problem and counseled to adhere to it. But we cannot expect that they will be able to engage in spiritual warfare as we know it.

We Are What We Think

The Bible spoke on this subject long ago, when Solomon said, "For as he thinketh in his heart, so is he." Countless self-help groups today discuss this concept. Leaders in the field of self-development build entire programs around it.

To illustrate the significance of this idea, suppose your biggest creditor—maybe your mortgage holder—called you into his office tomorrow and presented you with a statement stamped, "Paid in Full." How would you feel? Fantastic, right? But what if he informed you that he was demanding full payment right now, or you could go to jail? How would you feel about *that*? If you are like most people, you would feel *less* than happy . . . and understandably so.

Most of us are like that: our feelings change depending on the circumstances. Thus, we waste a tremendous amount of time and energy trying to manipulate our circumstances so we will *feel* better. That is well and good, up to a point. It is certainly normal to be concerned about paying our bills. And if there is something in our lives that is distressing, and we are in a position to change it, then by all means, let us change it. We should not put it off, but just do it!

All too often, however, we confront circumstances over which we have little or no control. Having an alcoholic husband is one example. We cannot count on improving our own emotional state by changing someone else.

Or perhaps we have a negative physical condition, such as a missing leg or arm. Maybe we have been evicted from our home because the owner just sold it to someone who is planning to move in. There will always be circumstances beyond our control. There will always be things we cannot change. Sometimes we go through times in life when it seems like *everything* is out of control. And it could very well be.

The story of Paul and Silas is an example. There was nothing they could do about being bound in stocks in a prison. But they knew a secret that we, too, can know. The secret is this:

The outside world may have control over your body, but nothing can control your mind unless you let it. You have complete control over what you choose to think about. No one but you can control how you react to your circumstances. When you truly understand this point, you will see a tremendous change in your life.

The way we usually proceed is as follows: A circumstance happens, which we will call C. Then we react; let us call our reaction R. Here are some examples:

C: "I get a raise."	➡	R: "I must be great!"
C: "I get fired."	➡	R: "I must be no good."
C: "My son is late."	➡	R: "He had a bad accident."

The first thing to notice about our reactions is that they are typically irrational. Clearly, there is some erroneous thinking. Something is missing, but what is it? We will find out in the next chapter.

Notes to Myself

CHAPTER ELEVEN

SELF-TALK

When I left my office the other day and walked to my car, I caught myself thinking, I'm starving! Well, I had just eaten lunch two hours ago, so there was no way I could be starving. As I scrambled into my car to head home, I caught this conversation with myself. How funny! I was frustrated with how things had turned out with a patient, and I was thinking a snack would make me feel better. Starving, indeed.

As I maneuvered through the traffic, I began telling myself that I was not even hungry, much less starving. Sure enough, before long my appetite was normal and I was thinking of things other than food. Pretty soon, though, I saw my favorite fast-food joint coming up. It seemed an automatic thing for my car to get into the lane to turn into the drive-through. I thought a quick snack would tide me over till I got home. (Home was twenty minutes away.)

Again, I caught this conversation inside my head and forced the car to go straight. "Self," I said, "you are not hungry."

Self said, "I need a snack. I'm getting weak!"

"You had lunch, self."

Self went on to say, "In fact, I'm even getting dizzy. That lunch I ate wasn't enough to feed a bird."

And that is how it goes.

How about you? Recall some recent battle you had with yourself, some choice or decision you needed to make. Can you remember how the conversation with yourself went?

In the conversation with myself that I just described, not only did I stop thinking about a certain thing, but I also put a substitute thought in its place. For example, "I'm starving" became "I'm not hungry."

If my subconscious mind can believe the lie that I am starving (and it *was* a lie because I decidedly was not starving), then it can also believe the truth—that I am not hungry. The subconscious mind does not discern the difference between truth and fiction, good and bad. It simply processes the statements we plug in.

Our last chapter concluded by asking, "What is missing?" The answer is, *our interpretation*. It is not the event; it is not the circumstance that produces the feeling. It is our interpretation of the event or circumstance. Getting a revelation of this concept has revolutionized my life.

If we but take the moment or two necessary to accomplish this step, we will begin to see real changes in the way we live. We will begin to see a more positive outlook develop in our thinking. We will see less gloom in the world around us. It is the truth. My own life testifies to it.

Antidotes to Negative Thinking

"Whatsoever things are true, whatsoever things are honest, whatsoever things are just, whatsoever things are pure, whatsoever things are lovely, whatsoever things are of good report; if there be any virtue, and if there be any praise, think on these things" (Philippians 4:8).

Philippians 4 lists several biblical attitudes necessary in conquering distorted thinking and winning over depression:

- "Rejoice in the Lord alway" (Philippians 4:4).
- Right praying (Philippians 4:6).
- Think list (Philippians 4:8).

Now is the time to think seriously about verse 8 and how we can apply it to our situation, to revolutionize our life. We need to chew it up and swallow it.

The Bible tells us to pray for our enemies and those who mistreat us. (See Matthew 5:44.) Do you find this hard to do? Most people do, but that does not negate the Scriptures. We must obey the Word of God. "To him that knoweth to do good, and doeth it not, to him it is sin" (James 4:17). As we have learned, unconfessed sin is a cause of depression.

Using Philippians 4:8, take a moment to think about the person whom you have the *hardest* time praying for. Think of at least *one good thing* about this person. With this good thing in mind, you can begin to pray for him or her. Concentrating on good memories of difficult people will help you to pray for them. So will reminding ourselves of their humanity and frailty, as in the example we gave of the wayward son wandering around on the street.

I was troubled once with a person at work. I honestly could not think of anything good about this person, as she harassed me endlessly, day after weary day. Once, when I had more time than she did, I tried to win her over by doing some of her typing for her. She tore it to shreds in front of the whole office, screaming in a loud voice that it was not done the way she wanted. I almost gave up on this person. But by applying this verse, I searched diligently for something—anything!—to latch onto. I went over and over Philippians 4:8.

Finally I happened to remember something about her, a special moment we had shared together. I paused to reflect on that moment. In my mind, I could see again the joy on her face and the laughter in her eye. I allowed myself to dwell on this picture of her. With that picture in my mind, I found it was not so hard to pray for her after all. And when we pray for others, something happens inside *us*.

No, she did not stop harassing me. But at least I had

a good, positive thought to lock into. Keeping that picture in my mind helped me to care enough to pray for her throughout the day, which meant I was keeping my mind on the Lord. Things will happen in our lives when we learn to pray for our enemies.

Something else occurs also. When we truly pray for our enemies, for those who have harmed us—when we pray and ask God to bless them as we ourselves would like to be blessed—something wonderful begins to happen. Not only do we begin to be healed, but also God will bring our enemies through the circumstances necessary for them to receive the blessings we pray down on them. In other words, vengeance truly does belong to the Lord.

A Little Dose of Ipecac

For every negative thing we can think about ourselves, there is an antidote. My favorite antidotes are passages of Scripture, because nobody can improve on what the Lord has to say about us! We need to have antidotes ready. They need to be in good repair and ready to use at a second's notice.

An antidote is a remedy designed to counteract a poison. More broadly speaking, according to Webster, an antidote is "anything that works against an evil." In this sense, ipecac is an antidote in the form of a syrup, for it is used to induce vomiting when someone has accidentally swallowed poison.

Let us take the example of your child swallowing some poison. You immediately call the doctor, but his answering service says it will be a while before he can get back to you. It is sixty-seven miles to the nearest hospital, and you do not know what to do. You pace back and forth, the kid's eyes are starting to droop, and the next-door neighbor, an old-fashioned grandmother of twenty-three, tells you to get out the ipecac.

At first you tell her you do not have any, but then you remember that there used to be a bottle of the stuff around somewhere. You tear through the house trying to find it. You race through the rooms and tear open the medicine chest, growing terrified that your child might expire any moment.

Ipecac is what you need in this case, but what good is it if you cannot find it? You have to be prepared!

Antidotes, in our discussion here, are thoughts that we will immediately substitute for the negative thoughts (poison) we will pull out of our mind. Another word we can use for them is affirmations. They are not used exclusively; they do not stand on their own. Affirmations or antidotes, as I like to call them, are used in conjunction with other things.

When you cut or dig out something, a hole is left. That hole must be filled with something. If you do not fill it immediately with good things, then negative things will return.

I keep stressing *immediately.* You have to work fast to replace your extracted thoughts. Many times, if you have to stop and search frantically for something good to substitute, the negative will flow back in again. Negative thoughts are like weeds that grow rapidly.

A good part of my professional life has been spent working with alcoholics. Here is a set of antidotes from rational-emotive therapy that I have used from time to time with alcoholics. Study them to see how you might change the words to apply to your own life.

Self-Defeating Thought: Not drinking is just too hard. I can't stand not having what I want.

Rational Alternative: While not drinking is certainly difficult, I have stood it for some time now, and one hour or one day at a time I can continue to stand it. I don't need everything I merely want, and while I may want a drink, I don't want all the problems that it will bring.

Self-Defeating Thought: I need more excitement in my life. I'm so bored. I'll go visit my friends at the bar but not take a drink.

Rational Alternative: Nobody ever died of boredom. While I certainly would like more excitement, the price of associating with my old friends might be drinking again. I'm not willing to pay that price.

Self-Defeating Thought: Poor me. Nothing is going right for me. What's the use?

Rational Alternative: While things may not be great now, it doesn't help to pity myself. It only makes me feel worse. I need to think through that drink I want. Remember that last drink? Did that make life better?

Self-Defeating Thought: I'm so upset. If I don't have a drink, I'll go crazy. I'd rather be drunk than crazy.

Rational Alternative: A drink won't prevent me from going crazy. In fact, it may take me further down the road. Being uptight can be best handled without a drink. *People don't go crazy from not getting what they want.*

It is imperative to gather together, in advance, your own antidotes to stock your medicine chest. Learn to recognize when feelings and emotions are controlling you. Focus on Scripture. "Thou wilt keep him in perfect peace, whose mind is stayed on thee" (Isaiah 26:3).

Record of Activities

A common complaint of depressed people is that there is no pleasure in living. This statement could be discouraging to hear, but it can also be a platform for showing the person that his thinking is messed up. Here is how.

I like to keep an activity record for a week, because a common problem is the tendency to use *selective thinking*. This means we forget the pleasant things that happen in our lives and remember the rest. We selectively screen out the good to concentrate on the bad and the not-so-good. To counteract this tendency, we can keep a record of our activities and then rate each of the activities as being pleasant or unpleasant (or any degree in between). When we review this record at the end of the week, we force ourselves to discover that our thinking has been leading us astray. There was indeed pleasure in our lives, and this record is proof that our thinking is distorted and need to be changed. Like the woman on the cold, rainy anniversary night, we can be defeated by generalized, distorted thinking.

Exposing the Destructive Core Belief

Practitioners of cognitive therapy agree that, in essence, an event produces a thought, the thought produces a feeling, and the feeling, in turn, produces a certain behavior. Here is an example: My pastor walked by me tonight without speaking to me (event). I thought, He does not really like me. My feeling: I am hurt, disappointed, and feel that I am not good enough. As a result, I decide to work harder to please him. The resulting behavior is one of trying harder to please my pastor so that he will like me. The problem is I had not displeased him in the first place; he simply did not see me when he passed, because he had just received some disturbing news and it was on his mind. So I am working hard to fix something that is not even broken. The result is going to be depression.

Often we need to do more than just change a thought, because as we dig deeper into our modes of thinking, we discover that the thoughts are automatic, based on a deep, core belief. We need to uncover the core belief in order to expose the underlying need. I tracked down an example from my own life of perfectionism with this result: my core belief was, *I am not loved and accepted unless I am perfect.* I had to annihilate this belief to be victorious. (And I am still working on it!)

In the example of my pastor not speaking to me, the core belief is what will ultimately lead to depression, with all the distorted thoughts paving the way. Basically the problem is this: I believe that the other saints are more spiritual than I. Therefore, I conclude, my pastor surely believes that they are more important than I. If I am not as spiritual, then I am not as good as the rest of them. That means I need to take on even *more* activities and must do even *more* for God. This kind of activity—perceived as the avenue to the perfection that is required if I am to be accepted and loved—will only end in frustration and more "failures." In this way, I am setting myself up for major depression!

The core belief (I am not loved and accepted unless I am perfect) leads to the thought (I am not as spiritual as the other members), which leads to the behavior (more activity), which leads to disappointing "failure." The core belief (which went back to my childhood when nothing I did seemed to please my mother) is what I must attack. This analysis does not mean we are to blame our parents, however. Typically, they did the best they could with what they had. It is our responsibility to change according to the light God gives us.

Saturating ourselves with the holy Word of God can have a dramatic, supernatural effect on us. Jesus said, "Ye are clean through the word which I have spoken to you" (John 15:3).

Do you want to be clean? Immerse yourself in His Word. Study the Word! Read the Word! Memorize the

Word! Meditate on the Word! Pray the Word! If you will do this and do it faithfully, you will see wonderful results in your life.

I once counseled a minister and his wife who would not follow these simple instructions. I assigned them a mere chapter a day for a week. They were not praying either, so I assigned them fifteen minutes of daily prayer. They returned week after week, having done neither. I do not want to work with people who do not believe the Bible, or who refuse to read it or to pray. This lovely preacher's wife, once used by God, has been committed to a mental institution.

When I first got this news I fell to my knees in sorrow. When I rose, I was more determined than ever to help people get into the Word and to pray! In the times in which we are living, if we do not do these things, Satan will get us. We are in warfare, and we cannot fight a war and win without our weapons. There is no discharge from this war—either we fight or we are slain as a casualty. I have been so worn down that all I wanted to do was roll over and play dead. But I cannot! The weapons of our warfare are not carnal. When Satan came against Jesus, Jesus fought each temptation with the Word of God, saying, "It is written. . . ." But we cannot just say those three words; we must know what is written!

I use a Bible study for counseling dedicated people who are determined to be healed. It gets people so deep into the Word of God that they are changed from within. I counseled one young woman who really loved the Word of God, and she began to study her assignments. Once she phoned me with this complaint: “Sister Allison, I don’t have to read all these verses of Scripture, do I?”

“Yep. All of them.”

“But I’ve read them so many times already, I know what they’re going to say before I even turn there!”

“Read all of them. I want you so immersed in God and His Word that it’s coming out your ears.”

“But why?”

“Because John 1 tells us that God’s Word is God. When God’s Word fills you to overflowing, you will be healed.”

She did, and she has become a strong saint of God, emotionally healed! I do not believe in counseling relationships that result in dependence on the counselor. That is why I teach those I counsel to depend on God and His Word.

CHAPTER TWELVE

DEMONIC OPPRESSION

At this point, let us discuss the possibility of demonic activity in cases of depression. We should not look for demons behind every tree. At the same time, we must realize that Satan is alive and well and working overtime, because he knows his time is short. If depression can be such an effective tool to snatch away God's children, we can be assured that Satan is using it in the world today.

Some years ago as I was in the early stages of first writing this book, my life suddenly fell apart. Again. (My life has a funny way of doing that from time to time.) Over a period of months, Murphy played havoc with my life—everything that could go wrong, did. Things were crashing in around me, and all of it was out of my control.

At that time it had been nineteen years since my husband divorced me for the other woman. During those years, I had gradually closed off my feelings and had been unable to really love another man. I had dedicated myself to serving God and was quite happy basing my life on I Corinthians 7:34. I had remained single, and it was very likely that I would continue to remain so.

As I approached my fiftieth birthday, however, something inside of me went bonkers, right along with all my hormones. My son had moved away, and I was left in the proverbial empty nest. I have not read anything on the empty nest syndrome and the *single* parent. As a single parent, all the usual things about renewing the marriage did not apply. A single parent can be more devastated than a married couple when that last child moves out.

I began to experience a loneliness that had never been troublesome before. I began to date again but, because of the hurt still in my heart, I picked men with whom I really could not fall in love—until a certain friend suddenly became a widower. A few months after his wife, who was also my friend, passed away, he and I met again at a birthday party for a mutual friend.

We began dating, and within a very short time, we fell in love. In spite of all my precautions, I let go of my heart. I fell very hard into a situation that became one of the most heartbreaking experiences of my life, because to marry this man was not the will of God. Upon our breakup, I was devastated. And Satan was there, of course, to take advantage of it. There I was in the old, familiar spiral, going down, down, down towards depression. Every sign was there that I was headed for full-blown depression. If my past behavior was any indicator, it would be soon, and it would be bad. Satan said, "See? Look at you! Who wants to be like *you?*"

Winter set in. The economy was dreadful. I lost my job. I ended up in the hospital with surgery. Financially, I found myself in deep distress, so when my water heater went out, I had no way to fix it. It had leaked and caused major water damage to my back bedroom. My furnace also went out. I was without heat or hot water and feeling darker and gloomier every day.

Satan said, "See? Look at you? Why don't you just tear up that stupid book you're doing on depression? Who do you think you are, trying to help someone else when you're so down yourself?"

When a person is already weakened, it is so easy to listen to the enemy. His words sound so plausible. He was beating me up with accusations and condemnation, and I was allowing it. During this period I went to church only because it was the thing to do, not because I really wanted to. I sat through services like an automaton, because by this time I was in the early stage of feeling sorry for myself.

But one night after service, everything changed. I was trying to make a beeline for the door, slink into my car, and head home. A young woman stopped me, her hand timidly on my sleeve. I turned and looked at her helplessly, on the verge of excusing myself. But there was a certain look in her eye, a look that said she needed help. Satan was working on this young woman and her family, and many souls were in the balance. I forced myself to focus on God as best as I could, mentally seeking His help, submitting myself and this woman's problem to Him.

Suddenly something rose up in me. I thought about this book and about the work I was trying to accomplish, work that I knew was God's will for me and for those I was trying to help. Even as I felt my face flush with shame at almost falling again into the awful trap of depression, I squared my shoulders and placed my arm around the young woman. I refused to accept the depression. I absolutely had no time for it. All the groundwork I had laid, as set forth in this book, had strengthened me. "Resist the devil, and he will flee from you" (James 4:7). I did not rebuke him. I did not engage in any kind of visible warfare. I simply resisted. And, true to the Word of God, Satan fled.

This experience illustrates an important truth: sometimes stumbling can keep you from falling. You stumble, you catch your balance, and you keep on going. You do not have to fall to the ground. I stumbled. I caught my balance, so to speak, and I went on with life.

As we learn to change our thinking, we learn that we can do it immediately. We can receive the benefits at once, just as with God's forgiveness. We do not have to spend long periods in remorse and penance. Even if we should fall all the way to the ground, we do not have to remain there! We can get up, shake the dust off, and get on with the program. God's plan is a beautiful plan. He designed it so we do not have to miss a lot of work—*His* work!

This brings me to another point. Prayer is the most important work we can do. Often, it is the *only* thing we can do. As we draw closer and closer to the end of this age, the importance of prayer becomes even greater. The enemy would do anything to stop our prayers. He cannot stand it when a child of God gets on her knees to pray. And as more and more of our brothers and sisters become spiritually incapacitated and unable to pray for themselves, we must stand in the gap and intercede for them. Yet how can we, if we are caught up in our own problems and our own feelings? How can we reach outside of ourselves and intercede for someone else when we are in pain and suffering? *Yet this is the very thing we must do.* Every moment spent in depression is a moment stolen away from the life-saving, soul-saving work of God.

I once had a pastor who struggled with depression. When I went to him for help, he gave me a prescription so simple that I almost did not even try it: Bake a cake for our evangelist. I could not even muster up the strength to boil an egg—*bake a cake*? But I did, and it worked. It always works when we get outside ourselves and focus on someone else. It is the devil's job to see that our spiritual eyes remain turned into ourselves. That short-circuits God's work.

When we suspect demonic depression, the first step is to obey the first statement of James 4:7: "Submit yourselves therefore to God." This can involve falling onto our knees and a good old-fashioned "praying through." With a conscious decision of our own wills, we turn our lives over anew to God. In my case, as I stood in the vestibule among a crowd of people, it was turning to God with a mental plea. We must realize that we are powerless against the enemy; we cannot fight him in the flesh. So we must turn our lives and our wills over to Jesus at once.

The second step is to obey the second statement of James 4:7: "Resist the devil, and he will flee from you." Resisting Satan is not the same as rebuking him or casting out demons. Rather, we must consciously oppose the methods that Satan uses to influence us.

God takes care of His children. We must trust in Him and look to Him when in doubt. We need to watch out for fear and other sinful thoughts, because they can open up the mind to invasion. It is absolutely imperative that we learn to keep our thoughts pure. The main thing is to continually monitor what is going inside our heads. If we allow ourselves to dwell on thoughts of lust and greed and fear, for example, we can expect such thoughts to multiply and mushroom on the battlefield of our minds. It is inevitable. What we sow, we shall reap. What we plant, we shall harvest.

When we are in a situation that is capable of weakening us, such as the one where my life fell apart while finishing this book, we must be especially wary. I had let my guard down and was susceptible to attack. Jesus said, "Watch and pray" (Matthew 26:41). We need to be forever watchful and vigilant. It is so easy, when things are going well, to relax.

When the Holy Spirit reveals to us an area in our lives that needs repentance, we must be careful not to become defensive. We must not quench the work of the Spirit. Instead we must truly repent. "Victory begins with the name of Jesus on your lips; but it will not be consummated until the nature of Jesus is in your heart. . . . Satan will be allowed to come against the area of your weakness until you realize God's only answer is to become Christ-like (Frangipane 1989, 8).

How can we determine if our depression is demonic in origin? It really does not matter. Regardless of the source, we need to respond the same way, by submitting to God and resisting the devil. When we are trained in cognitive techniques, we know how to change our thought patterns immediately. But we can ask some simple questions: How do we recognize the source of our thinking? Are these thoughts consistent with me? Would I really be thinking something like this? Or is it something completely alien to the way I think? Are these thoughts true? Are they consistent with Scripture? Are they base, or noble?

It is important to focus our minds on Jesus and to praise Him. We must cast down imaginations and bring every thought into captivity. (See II Corinthians 10:5.) Praise and thanksgiving can help cure depression no matter what the spiritual cause. They help get our minds onto Jesus and onto things that are consistent with Philippians 4:8.

The cure for demonic oppression is to be filled with the Holy Spirit. It is possible to receive the Holy Ghost and not be continually filled. For this reason, Ephesians 5:18 urges us, "Be filled with the Spirit." A glass can be clean and have pure water in it but still not be filled. We need to pray every day to be so full of the Spirit that our "glass" is overflowing. But even Spirit-filled children of

God can anticipate being troubled by the enemy. Acts 2:38 is only the beginning of our walk with God; it is not the ending. We must be ever vigilant, watchful. Most certainly, this includes our thought life.

The following is a list of goals for every day. It helps us to keep in touch with our feelings and thoughts on a daily basis.

Goals for Every Day

1. To identify a negative mood as it is starting and nip it in the bud.

2. To identify changes in my body that indicate stress.

3. To identify my negative thoughts and switch them with positive thoughts.

4. To learn to "eavesdrop" on conversation that goes on inside my head, and change the course of that conversation if I do not like what I am hearing.

5. To replace as many negative thoughts as I can with positive ones, and when I can't immediately think of one, begin quoting a Bible verse.

6. To be *patient* and *forgiving* with myself when I fail to do these things. I will try to remember that I am changing lifelong habits and that this will take time and effort—lots of it.

7. Learn to depend moment by moment on God. He is the One who will change me.

8. Accept that not all things *can* be changed. In those cases, I will try to learn to change the way I *interpret* those things.

CHAPTER THIRTEEN

WHEN ALL IS SAID AND DONE . . .

Counseling is a ministry. It is a work, a gift, given by God to help in the restoration of His creation. Counselors, then, whether in the form of professionals, pastors, or just plain concerned friends, are a gift from heaven. But there will come a time when other people, no matter how skilled, no matter how caring, simply cannot help. Those times, too, are sent by God to teach us to rely on Him, to help us see that He is our only true source.

There have been times in my own struggle when nothing I did seemed to help. I would pray. I would change my thoughts. I would examine myself for unconfessed sin or anger. And yet I remained depressed and felt myself slipping ever deeper into the depression. At these times there is nothing left to do but rest in Jesus, which is really what we should be doing anyway.

I, like so many others, find that these times are more and more frequent. The times when absolutely no one can help us seem to multiply. Everyone is racing in the fast lane. That is because of the times we are living in, and that is the reason that prayer must be our top priority.

Once as I was driving to work, the depression I was experiencing would not lift. I knew that ahead of me lay the problems of a house full of women alcoholics who depended on me for guidance and counseling and care. That is not the kind of job one can walk into while in a depressed state.

I drove along, praying, pulling up the proverbial bootstraps. Finally, I just turned to the Lord and said, "Lord Jesus, help. I just can't do it! Lift me, Lord, lift me out of this. I've done what I could; the rest is up to You." He never fails to answer such a prayer from the heart!

There will be times when it seems that we just cannot pray. On one occasion I lay in bed, totally overwhelmed by everything outside the walls of my bedroom. It would take more than sweet and wise words to restore me. I had no interest in anything. I had no motivation to worry about my thinking. I had no desire to try anything else to pull myself out of this awful pit of misery. Was there any hope for one such as I?

The hope, as always, lies in Jesus. I lay there motionless, shut my eyes, and with cool, stiff lips, whispered, "Jesus."

My faith rested solely in the name that is above all names. Every knee shall bow at that name. Every demon in hell is subject to that name. And that includes the demon of depression. Within two hours, I was back at my word processor, working away, caught up again in the wonderful world of the living!

And that is what He is there for. That is what grace is all about. We are never good enough. We are never worthy enough. But His mercy and His grace are what we need. Mark 11:22 says, "Have faith in God." It is not saying to trust in how much we pray or the number of days we fast. We are not to have faith in our own walk with God or in the good things we do. We are not to have faith in our burden. But we are to have faith in God.

Focus on God! Remember all the times He came through for you. Recall the favorite Bible stories of how He parted the Red Sea and fed the multitudes. Have faith in God. Just rest there quietly in Him. Do not try to make yourself do anything that might result in more condemnation. Rest in Him, focus your thinking on Him. Just have faith in God.

There will be times when we cannot pray and when our faith seems to fail us. At those times we must be prepared to trust in God. The more I speak to groups and deal with hurting people, the more I come to believe that God has a message for today: "Trust in the LORD with all your heart, and lean not on your own understanding" (Proverbs 3:5, NKJV).

Things are going to get worse in this world, if the Lord delays His coming for His children. We need to be prepared for whatever may come. The Lord may come tonight, He may come tomorrow, or He may delay His coming. The important thing is that we, like good soldiers, endure to the end, for those who do so will be saved. (See Matthew 10:22.) We must be ready for His coming every day. My husband and I have a plaque over our door that reads, "Today Perhaps."

Today perhaps. Yes, it could very well be. But if not, we must trust in Him. The things we see in the world around us now, though shocking and devastating, are but a tip of the iceberg to come. If we cannot trust Him now, in these times when we still have freedom in America, what will we do in a world of persecution? We need to learn to trust Him now.

When we truly trust God, we have peace—peace that passes all understanding. And when we have peace, depression has to flee. In its place comes joy.

Thoughts of Suicide

But what if, I hear some of you say? What if nothing works, and the only option left is that of suicide?

It is tragic that Christians would even consider suicide. Tragic or not, it is a very real thought. It is not really an option, but rather a place. Thoughts of suicide rest in a place of no hope. A depressed person becomes a candidate for suicide when and if he or she reaches this place of hopelessness. Christians do reach this place!

Denying that fact does not make it go away.

If you are confronted with this situation in someone else, please take it seriously. Do not make light of the feelings. Do not be afraid to talk about it. Do not be afraid to discuss the possibility.

A person in depression builds walls around her heart, walls that separate, walls that alienate others. That is why it is often difficult to communicate with depressed people, and so easy to give up trying to reach them. But do not give up. Never take them out of your prayers until they have been brought to safety. Always take them seriously.

How can a born-again child of God even consider suicide? A depressed person is not thinking normally and rationally. Things that are considered taboo in a normal state—such as ending one's own life—become viable realities when a person reaches the pits of depression. Thinking becomes clouded by pain and the desire to escape the pain.

One of my clients, a strong saint of God for twenty years, told me recently, "I've reached a place where I just can't go on."

"Tell me what you're feeling right now."

"I'm so afraid!"

"What is it you are afraid of?" I probed. It had taken me a moment to fully realize what she was saying.

"I'm just afraid . . . to go on living any longer."

The red flag was waving ninety miles an hour by now. It was time to get this dreaded thing out in the open. "You are afraid you might commit suicide?" She nodded. "How do you think you might do it?" Silence. "Pills?" Again she nodded.

Remember, do not be afraid to talk about the subject. If the person is considering suicide, it cannot do anything but good to bring it out in the open and talk about it. This is where so many helpers err, and become afraid and try to change the subject. That is not what the person needs. She needs to be able to talk about it. She needs a safe and supportive atmosphere, a person with a big ear and a closed mouth.

We prayed, we talked, and she left feeling a little better. I was not in a position to stay with her physically, but she remained in my prayers. Three days later she took an overdose. This lovely child of God actually did it! God was there for her and spared her life. But what if?

It does happen! This is the fear that most people have when encountering depression. Suicide is death and most people are not equipped to deal with death. People considering suicide need prayer more than anything, and they need emotional support as never before in their lives. Often, just having someone there who will stick like glue through it all is enough to help pull the person out.

Be prepared to spend a lot of time, if need be, with the person. Do not just pray with them and shoo them off. They need a safe place to be. God is the answer, but God uses people. Do not pray with someone unless you are willing to be a part of the answer. Praying does not necessarily mean that you will end up being inconvenienced, but it might. Be willing to love that person back to a place of safety! Look at that dear soul through eyes of compassion so that when she looks at you, she sees Jesus.

If you are suicidal, please be willing to reach out! One

of my biggest problems has been an inability to reach out. A pastor told me once, "Sister Lynda, you've got to learn to reach out to others for help."

"But I have to be strong. And I don't want to bother other people." (In my childhood I learned not to be a bother but just to keep quiet and out of the way.)

Reaching out can be a frightening proposition. First of all, it feels like an admission of weakness or lack of love for the Lord. McMinn answered this concern:

> Depression and hopelessness need not be seen as signs of weakness or lack of spirituality. Moses, Elijah, David, Paul, and other godly Bible characters experienced despair, even hopelessness. Perhaps God provides us with these examples to prepare us for our own times of discouragement. Hopelessness, like pain, causes us to look deeper into our faith, our world, and ourselves to find meaning (168).

What if the person you reach out to fails to respond and you end up feeling rejected? Sad to say, that is a very real possibility. What if you are rejected when you reach out to another human being, when you are already in the pit of rejection? Then please, suicidal child of God, reach out to someone else! *God has prepared someone's heart for you!* Do not quit reaching out until you find that person!

And please, saints of God, let us be kind to each other and love each other. We never know what a brother or sister is going through. Could it be that the lovely sister with the perfect hairdo and plastered-on smile, could she be thinking about suicide? Yes, it could be. So please, let us be sensitive to one another and guard our lips. Let us speak out love and healing to one another. We are living in the final hour, and the enemy's tricks are more deceptive, more vile, than ever. Let us watch out for one another!

In closing, let us return to the message of the book as stated in the preface. If you feel depressed . . . and even if you feel like ending your life . . . *it is okay to have these feelings.* It is not okay to end your life, and it is not okay to remain in the pit of depression. But it is okay to have these feelings.

God has allowed you to enter this place for a purpose. He knows where you are every second of every day. Nothing takes our almighty God by surprise. Nothing is too big for Him.

The Lord not only loved you enough to die for you, but He also loves you enough to stick with you through thick and thin. Let Him touch you. Let Him in! The saving, all-powerful name is only a breath away. Whisper it, whisper it right now: *Jesus* . . .

He will never turn away anyone who comes to Him. Would you turn away your own child who came sobbing to you? Neither will our God turn you away.

Jesus knows. . . .

"And him that cometh to me I will in no wise cast out."

—Jesus (John 6:37)

BIBLIOGRAPHY

Adams, Jay E. 1970. *Competent to Counsel.* Grand Rapids: Zondervan.

———. 1973. *Christian Counselor's Manual.* Grand Rapids: Zondervan.

Alcoholics Anonymous, 3d ed. 1976. *Big Book.* World Services.

Allison, Lynda. 1991. "The Quiet and Deadly Force." *The Vision* 22 (March, April, May 1991): 2-3.

Augsburger, David W. 1988. *The Freedom of Forgiveness.* Chicago: Moody.

Cook, William H. 1974. *Success, Motivation, and the Scriptures.* Nashville: Broadman Press.

Foster, Timothy. 1986. *Called to Counsel.* Nashville: Oliver-Nelson.

Frangipane, Francis. 1989. *The Three Battlegrounds.* Marion, IA.

Hansen, James C., Richard R. Stevic, and Richard W. Warner, Jr. 2d ed. 1977. *Counseling Theory and Process.* Boston: Allyn and Bacon.

Holy Bible, King James Version.

Lloyd-Jones, D. Martyn. 1965. *Spiritual Depression.* Grand Rapids, MI: Eerdmans.

Lovett, C. S. 1968. *Unequally Yoked Wives.* Baldwin Park, Cal.: Personal Christianity Publishers.

Mumford, Bob. 1971. *Take Another Look at Guidance.* Plainfield, N. J. Logos.

Seamands, David. 1981. *Healing for Damaged Emotions.* Wheaton: Victor Books.

About the Author

LINDA ALLISON DOTY is an overcomer, and it is her deepest desire to help others overcome. She says, "I can't remember a time when I was not depressed—I think I was born depressed! But we do not have to stay that way. It is the will of God for us to be delivered—healed of depression!" Her life attests to this truth, and she shares her own testimony within the pages of this book.

Lynda Doty received her Bachelor's and Master's degrees at Georgia State University. She studied clinical psychology and went on to complete her doctoral work through Evangel Christian University. She did her internship in Fresno County, California, and has been involved in counseling since 1973.

She has a special burden for the hurting, especially those suffering from depression, post-abortion syndrome, alcoholism, and abuse. Her methods center on the power of the Word of God, prayer, the anointing of the Holy Spirit, and His gifts.

Sister Doty is director of A Woman's Place, a healing ministry to "help women become all that God would have them be, by learning to examine themselves according to the Word of God and then working on those areas that do not measure up." A woman's place . . . is at the feet of Jesus!

Sister Doty evangelizes and speaks widely throughout the United States, teaching others how to apply the concepts of biblical counseling both in their own lives and in the lives of others. She often spends several days at a church, ministering to the congregation as a whole and then having individual sessions with people referred by the pastor. She also does special "Ladies' Days," teaching the power of godly thinking.

She is married to a minister who shares her burden for the hurting. George and Lynda Doty are currently associate ministers, assisting in a home mission work in Nebraska.

Other books by Sister Doty are *Help Me Heal, Walking in Trust, Lisa Said No, Larissa's Song, Goodbye, Granny Dix.*

Contact information:
PO Box 751
Beatrice, NE 68310
402-228-2025
E-mail: Hosanna@apostolic. net
Website: http://www.apostolic.net/awomansplace